This Journal Belongs To:

_____

the
mouth speaks
WHAT THE
heart
Luke 6:45
is full of.

Welcome, dear friends!

I am so glad you are here. You have been prayed for and sought after. You are embarking on a new journey with God, and I'm excited for you. My prayer for you is that you will learn to be delighted in God's Word and grow closer to Him daily. You will enjoy digging into God's Word, growing closer to Him, and experiencing His guidance in your life.

You will fall in love with the Lord as you get to know Him. You will realize what an awesome God He is, and worshipping the Lord will come easily to you. I can't wait for you to start planning, praying, and pushing.

Life will get in the way; things will happen that will make you question God. You will oversleep and be frustrated along the way, but plan to spend time with the Lord. When you run into problems, pray about this difficult time you are experiencing and push. Carve out time to spend with Him. Get up earlier and keep the prize in front of you. Take your Bible, and read (at least) one chapter. You will come out blessed!

You are not alone in this battle. We all battle life when we try to serve God. That is why I came up with these seven steps to read the Bible. Surprisingly, you can read most chapters in less than five minutes. After that, you can use the questions for deeper meditation.

God has good things in store for us.

Joshua 1:8

"This Book of the Law shall
not depart from your mouth,
but you shall meditate on it day and night,
so that you may be careful to do according to
all that is written in it.
For then you will make your way
prosperous, and then you will have good
success."

So How Do You Do It?

To read the Bible, you must make a simple plan and stick to it.

I give you the acronym K.I.S.S. to remember. It stands for: Keep it Simple, Silly!

Bible reading is not meant to be difficult. Make a simple plan. Even the Bible encourages us in Psalm 119:130 with the words "The unfolding of your words gives light; it imparts understanding to the simple." God's words will enlighten us and give us understanding.

The Bible is for simple people. You do not need to be a theologian to read it. God's Spirit will give us all we need.

.

Some K.I.S.S. Ideas to Help You Follow Through with Your Simple Plan

1. ...I can get up fifteen minutes earlier and read a minimum of a chapter in the Bible.
2. ...I can train myself to read the Bible before I watch TV (or bake cupcakes, sew a pillow, spend time on social media, play softball, etc.).
3. ...I can use my phone or tablet to listen to a chapter of the Bible every day. Try reading along as you listen. (I listen to whole books of the Bible when I'm driving.)
4. ...I can read my Bible before or after a meal.
5. ...I can read my Bible before I go to bed at night.

How Much Should I Read a Day?

People ask me how much they should read a day.

You can start where you are. There is no need to rush or push yourself too hard.

- You can read one chapter a day.

- You can break one chapter into two parts and read half chapter a day.

- You can follow my example. I read until I come across something that struck me, a wow or an aha moment. Then I stop and contemplate on it. I make notes in my devotional journal and plan to change my life to fit what I read that day.

So you see, there are no set rules on how you should read the Bible. Just start and see how the Holy Spirit leads you. He will help you grow.
I will be praying for you.

A Simple Plan for You

*For this devotional journal,
I suggest that you read one
chapter a day.
Most Bible books can be read in
less than a month. Here is a list
of books and chapters you can
choose from. Check them off when
you are done.*

New Testament

Book	# of Chapters	Yes I did it!
Matthew	28	
Mark	16	
Luke	24	
John	21	
Acts	28	
Romans	16	
1 Corinthians	16	
2 Corinthians	13	
Galatians	6	
Ephesians	6	
Philippians	4	
Colossians	4	
1 Thessalonians	5	
2 Thessalonians	3	
1 Timothy	6	
2 Timothy	4	
Titus	3	
Philemon	1	
Hebrews	13	
James	5	
1 Peter	5	
2 Peter	3	
1 John	5	
2 John	1	
3 John	1	
Jude	1	
Revelation	22	

Old Testament

Book	# of Chapters	Yes I did it!	Book	# of Chapters	Yes I did it!
Genesis	50		Ecclesiastes	12	
Exodus	40		Song of Songs	8	
Leviticus	27		Isaiah	66	
Numbers	36		Jeremiah	52	
Deuteronomy	34		Lamentations	5	
Joshua	24		Ezekiel	48	
Judges	21		Daniel	12	
Ruth	4		Hosea	14	
1 Samuel	31		Joel	3	
2 Samuel	24		Amos	9	
1 Kings	22		Obadiah	1	
2 Kings	25		Jonah	4	
1 Chronicles	29		Micah	7	
2 Chronicles	36		Nahum	3	
Ezra	10		Habakkuk	3	
Nehemiah	13		Zephaniah	3	
Esther	10		Haggai	2	
Job	42		Zechariah	14	
Psalms	150		Malachi	4	
Proverbs	31				

Books for Life
www.luisettekraal.com

Friends? Check me out on Facebook, Instagram. Share with me.

Attributes

of

God

1. God is a person	Praise God. He is not only a person but also my Abba father. My daddy. Gen.1 :26-27
2. God is Spirit	Praise God. I can worship in Spirit and in Truth. I can be in God's will today. John 1:18
3. God is unchanging	Praise God, God is not-changing. He cannot be holier, more merciful nor have more grace tomorrow. God is unchanging! Psalm 102
4. God is eternal	Praise God. I can praise God today and keep on until eternity. He is the everlasting God. Praise God. Psalm 119; Psalm 89; Psalm 90
5. God is all knowing	Praise God that I do not need to fret about the future. The God that is ALL KNOWING holds my future in His hands. Praise God. Psalm 139:1-6
6. God is everywhere	Praise God .... God is for us ... God is with us ... God is in us! Praise God. Psalm 139: 7-12

7. God is wise	Praise God, He is a wise God and wants to share this wisdom with me. Praise God. Romans 16:27
8. God is all powerful	Praise God, Even if we put all the powers in the world, nuclear, solar, hydroelectric, magnetic, satanic etc together, it would not begin to measure up to the omnipotence of God. Psalm 33:6-9
9. God is sovereign	Praise God, He is never out of control. 1 Chron. 29:11-14
10. God Is Holy	Praise God, there is no one holy as our God. Isa. 43:15
11. God is righteous	Praise God, our God is righteous. We can live by his will since He is a righteous God for us. Psalm 9:3-4
12. God is faithful and True	Praise God, even if I am unfaithful He remains faithful and true. Praise God I can focus on God's faithfulness and be saved from despair. Psalm 36:5
13. God is Love	Praise God, His love bought people free! Praise God for his everlasting love. 1 John 4:7
14. God is merciful	Praise God, He feels my misery and sends me help. 2 Cor. 1:3
15. God is gracious	Praise God, by grace He has given us salvation. 1 Peter 5:10
16. God is Good	Praise God. God is Good. His will for us are always good. Praise God He shows me his Goodness in saving me. Mark 10:18

LUISETTEKRAAL.COM

7 Step Devotional

The Bible: Passage & Date

-----/-----/-------

The New Thing

What is one new thing that stands out to you in today's passage?
It may be a verse you don't remember reading before.

The Wow Factor

What was the most important and impactful thing you read today? What made you say, "Wow! I'm blown away."

The Presence of Jesus in the Passage

What points to Jesus and His life in this passage? Does any verse remind you of something Jesus said or the way Jesus lived?

The Character of God

Who does God say that He is? Identify attributes from God's character in this passage. A good way to start, is to use words like: God is, God says, God does, God wants, or God can.

The 'So What' or the Next Steps

Now, ask yourself, 'So what?' If what you read is true, how will you apply this? What will you do differently? What has to change?

Time to Pray

It is time to pray and ask God to help you. Write down your prayer to God based on what you are learning from today's passage and questions.

How do you follow this devotional?

Pray and choose a Bible book to read.

(Any book is okay. They are all part of the Word of God.)

Begin from chapter 1

Read one (or more) chapter(s) a day.

Go deeper in your journal by following each one of the seven steps meticulously.

Pray.

(An example of this is on the next page.)

Example

Seven Steps Devotional Prayer Journal

1. The Bible: Passage_____ and Date_____

Example: Jeremiah 1

_01_ / _01_ / _2024_

2. The New Thing

What is one new thing that stands out to you in today's passage?
It may be a verse you don't remember reading before.

Example: In Jeremiah 1:5, I never realized that God knew a person before he was born. That is awesome.

3. The Wow Factor

What was the most important and impactful thing you read today? What made you say, "Wow! I'm blown away."

Example: In Jeremiah 1:7–8, God said to Jeremiah, "Do not say, 'I am too young.' You must go to everyone I send you to and say whatever I command you. Do not be afraid of their number, for I am with you and will rescue you." First of all, I did not know that Jeremiah was a young person. Prophet Jeremiah sounds so old to me. But the most amazing thing was that God tells him that it didn't matter that he was so young and that God Himself would give him the words to speak. Love it!

4. The Presence of Jesus in the Passage

What points to Jesus and His life in this passage? Does any verse remind you of something Jesus said or the way Jesus lived?

Example: In the New Testament, we see that the "Word of God" refers to Jesus. In this text, we read that the Word of God came to Jeremiah on several occasions. This reminds me of Jesus coming to bring the Good News.

5. The Character of God

Who does God say that He is? Identify attributes from God's character in this passage. A good way to start, is to use words like: God is, God says, God does, God wants, or God can.
Review your previous answers.

Example:
Verse 5: God speaks
Verse 17: The Lord commands
Verse 18: The Lord makes
Verse 19: God is with people
Verse 19: The Lord delivers

6. The 'So What' or the Next Steps

Now, ask yourself, 'So what?' If what you read is true, how will you apply this? What will you do differently? What has to change?

Example:
If all this is true, then it means that God knew me before I was born
and that he can change me and help me be a person who speaks. I like that
ideal I will be more interested to learn to speak to people now. I will ask
God to take away the feeling of being afraid or shy from me so I can
speak in front of people without fidgeting.

7. Time to Pray

It is time to pray and ask God to help you. Write down your prayer to God based on what you are learning from today's passage and questions.

Example: Today, I prayed about being able to speak to the children's ministry director
and telling her that I want to be part of the team. I also prayed for the courage to share
Christ with my coworkers.

1. The Bible: Passage_____ and Date_____

_____/_____/_____

2. The New Thing

What is one new thing that stands out to you in today's passage?
It may be a verse you don't remember reading before.

3. The Wow Factor

What was the most important and impactful thing you read today? What made you say, "Wow! I'm blown away."

4. The Presence of Jesus in the Passage

What points to Jesus and His life in this passage? Does any verse remind you of something Jesus said or the way Jesus lived?

5. The Character of God

Who does God say that He is? Identify attributes from God's character in this passage. A good way to start, is to use words like: God is, God says, God does, God wants, or God can.
Review your previous answers.

6. The 'So What' or the Next Steps

Now, ask yourself, 'So what?' If what you read is true, how will you apply this? What will you do differently? What has to change?

7. Time to Pray

It is time to pray and ask God to help you. Write down your prayer to God based on what you are learning from today's passage and questions.

1. The Bible: Passage_____ and Date_____

_____/_____/_____

2. The New Thing

What is one new thing that stands out to you in today's passage?
It may be a verse you don't remember reading before.

3. The Wow Factor

What was the most important and impactful thing you read today? What made you say, "Wow! I'm blown away."

4. The Presence of Jesus in the Passage

What points to Jesus and His life in this passage? Does any verse remind you of something Jesus said or the way Jesus lived?

5. The Character of God

Who does God say that He is? Identify attributes from God's character in this passage. A good way to start, is to use words like: God is, God says, God does, God wants, or God can.
Review your previous answers.

6. The 'So What' or the Next Steps

Now, ask yourself, 'So what?' If what you read is true, how will you apply this? What will you do differently? What has to change?

7. Time to Pray

It is time to pray and ask God to help you. Write down your prayer to God based on what you are learning from today's passage and questions.

1. The Bible: Passage_____ and Date_____

_____/_____/_____

2. The New Thing

What is one new thing that stands out to you in today's passage?
It may be a verse you don't remember reading before.

3. The Wow Factor

What was the most important and impactful thing you read today? What made you say, "Wow! I'm blown away."

4. The Presence of Jesus in the Passage

What points to Jesus and His life in this passage? Does any verse remind you of something Jesus said or the way Jesus lived?

5. The Character of God

Who does God say that He is? Identify attributes from God's character in this passage. A good way to start, is to use words like: God is, God says, God does, God wants, or God can.
Review your previous answers.

6. The 'So What' or the Next Steps

Now, ask yourself, 'So what?' If what you read is true, how will you apply this? What will you do differently? What has to change?

7. Time to Pray

It is time to pray and ask God to help you. Write down your prayer to God based on what you are learning from today's passage and questions.

1. The Bible: Passage_____ and Date_____

_____/_____/_____

2. The New Thing

What is one new thing that stands out to you in today's passage?
It may be a verse you don't remember reading before.

3. The Wow Factor

What was the most important and impactful thing you read today? What made you say, "Wow! I'm blown away."

4. The Presence of Jesus in the Passage

What points to Jesus and His life in this passage? Does any verse remind you of something Jesus said or the way Jesus lived?

5. The Character of God

Who does God say that He is? Identify attributes from God's character in this passage. A good way to start, is to use words like: God is, God says, God does, God wants, or God can.
Review your previous answers.

6. The 'So What' or the Next Steps

Now, ask yourself, 'So what?' If what you read is true, how will you apply this? What will you do differently? What has to change?

7. Time to Pray

It is time to pray and ask God to help you. Write down your prayer to God based on what you are learning from today's passage and questions.

1. The Bible: Passage_____ and Date_____

_____/_____/_____

2. The New Thing

What is one new thing that stands out to you in today's passage?
It may be a verse you don't remember reading before.

3. The Wow Factor

What was the most important and impactful thing you read today? What made you say, "Wow! I'm blown away."

4. The Presence of Jesus in the Passage

What points to Jesus and His life in this passage? Does any verse remind you of something Jesus said or the way Jesus lived?

5. The Character of God

Who does God say that He is? Identify attributes from God's character in this passage. A good way to start, is to use words like: God is, God says, God does, God wants, or God can.
Review your previous answers.

6. The 'So What' or the Next Steps

Now, ask yourself, 'So what?' If what you read is true, how will you apply this? What will you do differently? What has to change?

7. Time to Pray

It is time to pray and ask God to help you. Write down your prayer to God based on what you are learning from today's passage and questions.

Psalm 91

Those who live in the shelter of the Most High will find rest in the shadow of the Almighty. This I declare about the Lord: He alone is my refuge, my place of safety; he is my God, and I trust him. For he will rescue you from every trap and protect you from deadly disease. He will cover you with his feathers. He will shelter you with his wings. His faithful promises are your armor and protection. Do not be afraid of the terrors of the night, nor the arrow that flies in the day. Do not dread the disease that stalks in darkness, nor the disaster that strikes at midday. Though a thousand fall at your side, though ten thousand are dying around you, these evils will not touch you. Just open your eyes, and see how the wicked are punished. If you make the Lord your refuge, if you make the Most High your shelter, no evil will conquer you; no plague will come near your home. For he will order his angels to protect you wherever you go. They will hold you up with their hands so you won't even hurt your foot on a stone. You will trample upon lions and cobras; you will crush fierce lions and serpents under your feet! The Lord says, "I will rescue those who love me. I will protect those who trust in my name. When they call on me, I will answer; I will be with them in trouble. I will rescue and honor them. I will reward them with a long life and give them my salvation."

Prayers

1. The Bible: Passage_____ and Date_____

_____/_____/_____

2. The New Thing

What is one new thing that stands out to you in today's passage?
It may be a verse you don't remember reading before.

3. The Wow Factor

What was the most important and impactful thing you read today? What made you say, "Wow! I'm blown away."

4. The Presence of Jesus in the Passage

What points to Jesus and His life in this passage? Does any verse remind you of something Jesus said or the way Jesus lived?

5. The Character of God

Who does God say that He is? Identify attributes from God's character in this passage. A good way to start, is to use words like: God is, God says, God does, God wants, or God can.
Review your previous answers.

6. The 'So What' or the Next Steps

Now, ask yourself, 'So what?' If what you read is true, how will you apply this? What will you do differently? What has to change?

7. Time to Pray

It is time to pray and ask God to help you. Write down your prayer to God based on what you are learning from today's passage and questions.

1. The Bible: Passage_____ and Date_____

_____/_____/_____

2. The New Thing

What is one new thing that stands out to you in today's passage?
It may be a verse you don't remember reading before.

3. The Wow Factor

What was the most important and impactful thing you read today? What made you say, "Wow! I'm blown away."

4. The Presence of Jesus in the Passage

What points to Jesus and His life in this passage? Does any verse remind you of something Jesus said or the way Jesus lived?

5. The Character of God

Who does God say that He is? Identify attributes from God's character in this passage. A good way to start, is to use words like: God is, God says, God does, God wants, or God can.
Review your previous answers.

6. The 'So What' or the Next Steps

Now, ask yourself, 'So what?' If what you read is true, how will you apply this? What will you do differently? What has to change?

7. Time to Pray

It is time to pray and ask God to help you. Write down your prayer to God based on what you are learning from today's passage and questions.

1. The Bible: Passage_____ and Date_____

_____/_____/_____

2. The New Thing

What is one new thing that stands out to you in today's passage?
It may be a verse you don't remember reading before.

3. The Wow Factor

What was the most important and impactful thing you read today? What made you say, "Wow! I'm blown away."

4. The Presence of Jesus in the Passage

What points to Jesus and His life in this passage? Does any verse remind you of something Jesus said or the way Jesus lived?

5. The Character of God

Who does God say that He is? Identify attributes from God's character in this passage. A good way to start, is to use words like: God is, God says, God does, God wants, or God can.
Review your previous answers.

6. The 'So What' or the Next Steps

Now, ask yourself, 'So what?' If what you read is true, how will you apply this? What will you do differently? What has to change?

7. Time to Pray

It is time to pray and ask God to help you. Write down your prayer to God based on what you are learning from today's passage and questions.

1. The Bible: Passage_____ and Date_____

_____/_____/_____

2. The New Thing

What is one new thing that stands out to you in today's passage?
It may be a verse you don't remember reading before.

3. The Wow Factor

What was the most important and impactful thing you read today? What made you say, "Wow! I'm blown away."

4. The Presence of Jesus in the Passage

What points to Jesus and His life in this passage? Does any verse remind you of something Jesus said or the way Jesus lived?

5. The Character of God

Who does God say that He is? Identify attributes from God's character in this passage. A good way to start, is to use words like: God is, God says, God does, God wants, or God can.
Review your previous answers.

6. The 'So What' or the Next Steps

Now, ask yourself, 'So what?' If what you read is true, how will you apply this? What will you do differently? What has to change?

7. Time to Pray

It is time to pray and ask God to help you. Write down your prayer to God based on what you are learning from today's passage and questions.

1. The Bible: Passage_____ and Date_____

_____/_____/_____

2. The New Thing

What is one new thing that stands out to you in today's passage?
It may be a verse you don't remember reading before.

3. The Wow Factor

What was the most important and impactful thing you read today? What made you say, "Wow! I'm blown away."

4. The Presence of Jesus in the Passage

What points to Jesus and His life in this passage? Does any verse remind you of something Jesus said or the way Jesus lived?

5. The Character of God

Who does God say that He is? Identify attributes from God's character in this passage. A good way to start, is to use words like: God is, God says, God does, God wants, or God can.
Review your previous answers.

6. The 'So What' or the Next Steps

Now, ask yourself, 'So what?' If what you read is true, how will you apply this? What will you do differently? What has to change?

7. Time to Pray

It is time to pray and ask God to help you. Write down your prayer to God based on what you are learning from today's passage and questions.

NEW TESTAMENT

```
M D 2 D M J D M U Y P H I L E M O N
Y A N H U Q E P 1 A J O H N P L P Y
H B T D C O A H Y L C L E N N R B S
T J E T N O M I N K M H Q J H A T N
O S T V H O R L N V G Y B F O V A A
M U K L S E W I T H C H N O J X S I
I T P V W U W P N E N T E K Q N N N
T I Z W E E 2 P S T D O W L 3 G A O
B T R F R D A I S G H M L Z G U I L
2 K O Q B J J A E X P I J O H N S A
Q F M G E E O N M Q V T A Q Q C E S
R R A H H K S A C X T U N I H H S
E E N F N U N G J A P 1 U F S B P E
T T S C O L O S S I A N S Y Q U E H
E E Y M W G R E V E L A T I O N X T
P P R 1 A C O R I N T H I A N S U X
S J 1 H T H E S S A L O N I A N S 2
1 2 M A R K P G A L A T I A N S R M
```

MATTHEW
MARK
LUKE
JOHN
ROMANS
1 CORINTHIANS
2 CORINTHIANS
GALATIANS
EPHESIANS
PHILIPPIANS
COLOSSIANS
1 THESSALONIANS
2 THESSALONIANS
1 TIMOTHY
2 TIMOTHY
TITUS
PHILEMON
HEBREWS
JAMES

1 PETER   3 JOHN
2 PETER   JUDE
1 JOHN   REVELATION
2 JOHN

Where
GOD
guides,
He Provides.
ISAIAH 58:11

1. The Bible: Passage_____ and Date_____

_____/_____/_____

2. The New Thing

What is one new thing that stands out to you in today's passage?
It may be a verse you don't remember reading before.

3. The Wow Factor

What was the most important and impactful thing you read today? What made you say, "Wow! I'm blown away."

4. The Presence of Jesus in the Passage

What points to Jesus and His life in this passage? Does any verse remind you of something Jesus said or the way Jesus lived?

5. The Character of God

Who does God say that He is? Identify attributes from God's character in this passage. A good way to start, is to use words like: God is, God says, God does, God wants, or God can.
Review your previous answers.

6. The 'So What' or the Next Steps

Now, ask yourself, 'So what?' If what you read is true, how will you apply this? What will you do differently? What has to change?

7. Time to Pray

It is time to pray and ask God to help you. Write down your prayer to God based on what you are learning from today's passage and questions.

1. The Bible: Passage_____ and Date_____

_____/_____/_____

2. The New Thing

What is one new thing that stands out to you in today's passage?
It may be a verse you don't remember reading before.

3. The Wow Factor

What was the most important and impactful thing you read today? What made you say, "Wow! I'm blown away."

4. The Presence of Jesus in the Passage

What points to Jesus and His life in this passage? Does any verse remind you of something Jesus said or the way Jesus lived?

5. The Character of God

Who does God say that He is? Identify attributes from God's character in this passage. A good way to start, is to use words like: God is, God says, God does, God wants, or God can.
Review your previous answers.

6. The 'So What' or the Next Steps

Now, ask yourself, 'So what?' If what you read is true, how will you apply this? What will you do differently? What has to change?

7. Time to Pray

It is time to pray and ask God to help you. Write down your prayer to God based on what you are learning from today's passage and questions.

1. The Bible: Passage_____ and Date_____

_____/_____/_____

2. The New Thing

What is one new thing that stands out to you in today's passage?
It may be a verse you don't remember reading before.

3. The Wow Factor

What was the most important and impactful thing you read today? What made you say, "Wow! I'm blown away."

4. The Presence of Jesus in the Passage

What points to Jesus and His life in this passage? Does any verse remind you of something Jesus said or the way Jesus lived?

5. The Character of God

Who does God say that He is? Identify attributes from God's character in this passage. A good way to start, is to use words like: God is, God says, God does, God wants, or God can.
Review your previous answers.

6. The 'So What' or the Next Steps

Now, ask yourself, 'So what?' If what you read is true, how will you apply this? What will you do differently? What has to change?

7. Time to Pray

It is time to pray and ask God to help you. Write down your prayer to God based on what you are learning from today's passage and questions.

1. The Bible: Passage_____ and Date_____

_____/_____/_____

2. The New Thing

What is one new thing that stands out to you in today's passage?
It may be a verse you don't remember reading before.

3. The Wow Factor

What was the most important and impactful thing you read today? What made you say, "Wow! I'm blown away."

4. The Presence of Jesus in the Passage

What points to Jesus and His life in this passage? Does any verse remind you of something Jesus said or the way Jesus lived?

5. The Character of God

Who does God say that He is? Identify attributes from God's character in this passage. A good way to start, is to use words like: God is, God says, God does, God wants, or God can.
Review your previous answers.

6. The 'So What' or the Next Steps

Now, ask yourself, 'So what?' If what you read is true, how will you apply this? What will you do differently? What has to change?

7. Time to Pray

It is time to pray and ask God to help you. Write down your prayer to God based on what you are learning from today's passage and questions.

1. The Bible: Passage_____ and Date_____

_____/_____/_____

2. The New Thing

What is one new thing that stands out to you in today's passage?
It may be a verse you don't remember reading before.

3. The Wow Factor

What was the most important and impactful thing you read today? What made you say, "Wow! I'm blown away."

4. The Presence of Jesus in the Passage

What points to Jesus and His life in this passage? Does any verse remind you of something Jesus said or the way Jesus lived?

5. The Character of God

Who does God say that He is? Identify attributes from God's character in this passage. A good way to start, is to use words like: God is, God says, God does, God wants, or God can.
Review your previous answers.

6. The 'So What' or the Next Steps

Now, ask yourself, 'So what?' If what you read is true, how will you apply this? What will you do differently? What has to change?

7. Time to Pray

It is time to pray and ask God to help you. Write down your prayer to God based on what you are learning from today's passage and questions.

BEST
PRAYERS

OF MY
LIFE

IN THE morning
when I rise
GIVE me
Jesus.

1. The Bible: Passage_____ and Date_____

_____/_____/_____

2. The New Thing

What is one new thing that stands out to you in today's passage?
It may be a verse you don't remember reading before.

3. The Wow Factor

What was the most important and impactful thing you read today? What made you say, "Wow! I'm blown away."

4. The Presence of Jesus in the Passage

What points to Jesus and His life in this passage? Does any verse remind you of something Jesus said or the way Jesus lived?

5. The Character of God

Who does God say that He is? Identify attributes from God's character in this passage. A good way to start, is to use words like: God is, God says, God does, God wants, or God can.
Review your previous answers.

6. The 'So What' or the Next Steps

Now, ask yourself, 'So what?' If what you read is true, how will you apply this? What will you do differently? What has to change?

7. Time to Pray

It is time to pray and ask God to help you. Write down your prayer to God based on what you are learning from today's passage and questions.

1. The Bible: Passage_____ and Date_____

_____/_____/_____

2. The New Thing

What is one new thing that stands out to you in today's passage?
It may be a verse you don't remember reading before.

3. The Wow Factor

What was the most important and impactful thing you read today? What made you say, "Wow! I'm blown away."

4. The Presence of Jesus in the Passage

What points to Jesus and His life in this passage? Does any verse remind you of something Jesus said or the way Jesus lived?

5. The Character of God

Who does God say that He is? Identify attributes from God's character in this passage. A good way to start, is to use words like: God is, God says, God does, God wants, or God can.
Review your previous answers.

6. The 'So What' or the Next Steps

Now, ask yourself, 'So what?' If what you read is true, how will you apply this? What will you do differently? What has to change?

7. Time to Pray

It is time to pray and ask God to help you. Write down your prayer to God based on what you are learning from today's passage and questions.

1. The Bible: Passage_____ and Date_____

_____/_____/_____

2. The New Thing

What is one new thing that stands out to you in today's passage?
It may be a verse you don't remember reading before.

3. The Wow Factor

What was the most important and impactful thing you read today? What made you say, "Wow! I'm blown away."

4. The Presence of Jesus in the Passage

What points to Jesus and His life in this passage? Does any verse remind you of something Jesus said or the way Jesus lived?

5. The Character of God

Who does God say that He is? Identify attributes from God's character in this passage. A good way to start, is to use words like: God is, God says, God does, God wants, or God can.
Review your previous answers.

6. The 'So What' or the Next Steps

Now, ask yourself, 'So what?' If what you read is true, how will you apply this? What will you do differently? What has to change?

7. Time to Pray

It is time to pray and ask God to help you. Write down your prayer to God based on what you are learning from today's passage and questions.

1. The Bible: Passage_____ and Date_____

_____/_____/_____

2. The New Thing

What is one new thing that stands out to you in today's passage?
It may be a verse you don't remember reading before.

3. The Wow Factor

What was the most important and impactful thing you read today? What made you say, "Wow! I'm blown away."

4. The Presence of Jesus in the Passage

What points to Jesus and His life in this passage? Does any verse remind you of something Jesus said or the way Jesus lived?

5. The Character of God

Who does God say that He is? Identify attributes from God's character in this passage. A good way to start, is to use words like: God is, God says, God does, God wants, or God can.
Review your previous answers.

6. The 'So What' or the Next Steps

Now, ask yourself, 'So what?' If what you read is true, how will you apply this? What will you do differently? What has to change?

7. Time to Pray

It is time to pray and ask God to help you. Write down your prayer to God based on what you are learning from today's passage and questions.

1. The Bible: Passage_____ and Date_____

_____/_____/_____

2. The New Thing

What is one new thing that stands out to you in today's passage?
It may be a verse you don't remember reading before.

3. The Wow Factor

What was the most important and impactful thing you read today? What made you say, "Wow! I'm blown away."

4. The Presence of Jesus in the Passage

What points to Jesus and His life in this passage? Does any verse remind you of something Jesus said or the way Jesus lived?

5. The Character of God

Who does God say that He is? Identify attributes from God's character in this passage. A good way to start, is to use words like: God is, God says, God does, God wants, or God can.
Review your previous answers.

6. The 'So What' or the Next Steps

Now, ask yourself, 'So what?' If what you read is true, how will you apply this? What will you do differently? What has to change?

7. Time to Pray

It is time to pray and ask God to help you. Write down your prayer to God based on what you are learning from today's passage and questions.

your grace *is* SUFFICIENT.

2 Corinthians 12:9

Prayers

1. The Bible: Passage_____ and Date_____

_____/_____/_____

2. The New Thing

What is one new thing that stands out to you in today's passage?
It may be a verse you don't remember reading before.

3. The Wow Factor

What was the most important and impactful thing you read today? What made you say, "Wow! I'm blown away."

4. The Presence of Jesus in the Passage

What points to Jesus and His life in this passage? Does any verse remind you of something Jesus said or the way Jesus lived?

5. The Character of God

Who does God say that He is? Identify attributes from God's character in this passage. A good way to start, is to use words like: God is, God says, God does, God wants, or God can.
Review your previous answers.

6. The 'So What' or the Next Steps

Now, ask yourself, 'So what?' If what you read is true, how will you apply this? What will you do differently? What has to change?

7. Time to Pray

It is time to pray and ask God to help you. Write down your prayer to God based on what you are learning from today's passage and questions.

1. The Bible: Passage_____ and Date_____

_____/_____/_____

2. The New Thing

What is one new thing that stands out to you in today's passage?
It may be a verse you don't remember reading before.

3. The Wow Factor

What was the most important and impactful thing you read today? What made you say, "Wow! I'm blown away."

4. The Presence of Jesus in the Passage

What points to Jesus and His life in this passage? Does any verse remind you of something Jesus said or the way Jesus lived?

5. The Character of God

Who does God say that He is? Identify attributes from God's character in this passage. A good way to start, is to use words like: God is, God says, God does, God wants, or God can.
Review your previous answers.

6. The 'So What' or the Next Steps

Now, ask yourself, 'So what?' If what you read is true, how will you apply this? What will you do differently? What has to change?

7. Time to Pray

It is time to pray and ask God to help you. Write down your prayer to God based on what you are learning from today's passage and questions.

1. The Bible: Passage_____ and Date_____

_____/_____/_____

2. The New Thing

What is one new thing that stands out to you in today's passage?
It may be a verse you don't remember reading before.

3. The Wow Factor

What was the most important and impactful thing you read today? What made you say, "Wow! I'm blown away."

4. The Presence of Jesus in the Passage

What points to Jesus and His life in this passage? Does any verse remind you of something Jesus said or the way Jesus lived?

5. The Character of God

Who does God say that He is? Identify attributes from God's character in this passage. A good way to start, is to use words like: God is, God says, God does, God wants, or God can.
Review your previous answers.

6. The 'So What' or the Next Steps

Now, ask yourself, 'So what?' If what you read is true, how will you apply this? What will you do differently? What has to change?

7. Time to Pray

It is time to pray and ask God to help you. Write down your prayer to God based on what you are learning from today's passage and questions.

1. The Bible: Passage_____ and Date_____

_____/_____/_____

2. The New Thing

What is one new thing that stands out to you in today's passage?
It may be a verse you don't remember reading before.

3. The Wow Factor

What was the most important and impactful thing you read today? What made you say, "Wow! I'm blown away."

4. The Presence of Jesus in the Passage

What points to Jesus and His life in this passage? Does any verse remind you of something Jesus said or the way Jesus lived?

5. The Character of God

Who does God say that He is? Identify attributes from God's character in this passage. A good way to start, is to use words like: God is, God says, God does, God wants, or God can.
Review your previous answers.

6. The 'So What' or the Next Steps

Now, ask yourself, 'So what?' If what you read is true, how will you apply this? What will you do differently? What has to change?

7. Time to Pray

It is time to pray and ask God to help you. Write down your prayer to God based on what you are learning from today's passage and questions.

1. The Bible: Passage_____ and Date_____

_____/_____/_____

2. The New Thing

What is one new thing that stands out to you in today's passage?
It may be a verse you don't remember reading before.

3. The Wow Factor

What was the most important and impactful thing you read today? What made you say, "Wow! I'm blown away."

4. The Presence of Jesus in the Passage

What points to Jesus and His life in this passage? Does any verse remind you of something Jesus said or the way Jesus lived?

5. The Character of God

Who does God say that He is? Identify attributes from God's character in this passage. A good way to start, is to use words like: God is, God says, God does, God wants, or God can.
Review your previous answers.

6. The 'So What' or the Next Steps

Now, ask yourself, 'So what?' If what you read is true, how will you apply this? What will you do differently? What has to change?

7. Time to Pray

It is time to pray and ask God to help you. Write down your prayer to God based on what you are learning from today's passage and questions.

BEST
PRAYERS

OF MY

LIFE

Ephesians 3:14–19

Prayer for spiritual strength

When I think of all this, I fall to my knees and pray to the Father, the Creator of everything in heaven and on earth. I pray that from his glorious, unlimited resources he will empower you with inner strength through his Spirit. Then Christ will make his home in your hearts as you trust in him. Your roots will grow down into God's love and keep you strong. And may you have the power to understand, as all God's people should, how wide, how long, how high, and how deep his love is. May you experience the love of Christ, though it is too great to understand fully. Then you will be made complete with all the fullness of life and power that comes from God.

1. The Bible: Passage_____ and Date_____

_____/_____/_____

2. The New Thing

What is one new thing that stands out to you in today's passage?
It may be a verse you don't remember reading before.

3. The Wow Factor

What was the most important and impactful thing you read today? What made you say, "Wow! I'm blown away."

4. The Presence of Jesus in the Passage

What points to Jesus and His life in this passage? Does any verse remind you of something Jesus said or the way Jesus lived?

5. The Character of God

Who does God say that He is? Identify attributes from God's character in this passage. A good way to start, is to use words like: God is, God says, God does, God wants, or God can.
Review your previous answers.

6. The 'So What' or the Next Steps

Now, ask yourself, 'So what?' If what you read is true, how will you apply this? What will you do differently? What has to change?

7. Time to Pray

It is time to pray and ask God to help you. Write down your prayer to God based on what you are learning from today's passage and questions.

1. The Bible: Passage_____ and Date_____

_____/_____/_____

2. The New Thing

What is one new thing that stands out to you in today's passage?
It may be a verse you don't remember reading before.

3. The Wow Factor

What was the most important and impactful thing you read today? What made you say, "Wow! I'm blown away."

4. The Presence of Jesus in the Passage

What points to Jesus and His life in this passage? Does any verse remind you of something Jesus said or the way Jesus lived?

5. The Character of God

Who does God say that He is? Identify attributes from God's character in this passage. A good way to start, is to use words like: God is, God says, God does, God wants, or God can.
Review your previous answers.

6. The 'So What' or the Next Steps

Now, ask yourself, 'So what?' If what you read is true, how will you apply this? What will you do differently? What has to change?

7. Time to Pray

It is time to pray and ask God to help you. Write down your prayer to God based on what you are learning from today's passage and questions.

1. The Bible: Passage_____ and Date_____

_____/_____/_____

2. The New Thing

What is one new thing that stands out to you in today's passage?
It may be a verse you don't remember reading before.

3. The Wow Factor

What was the most important and impactful thing you read today? What made you say, "Wow! I'm blown away."

4. The Presence of Jesus in the Passage

What points to Jesus and His life in this passage? Does any verse remind you of something Jesus said or the way Jesus lived?

5. The Character of God

Who does God say that He is? Identify attributes from God's character in this passage. A good way to start, is to use words like: God is, God says, God does, God wants, or God can.
Review your previous answers.

6. The 'So What' or the Next Steps

Now, ask yourself, 'So what?' If what you read is true, how will you apply this? What will you do differently? What has to change?

7. Time to Pray

It is time to pray and ask God to help you. Write down your prayer to God based on what you are learning from today's passage and questions.

1. The Bible: Passage_____ and Date_____

_____/_____/_____

2. The New Thing

What is one new thing that stands out to you in today's passage?
It may be a verse you don't remember reading before.

3. The Wow Factor

What was the most important and impactful thing you read today? What made you say, "Wow! I'm blown away."

4. The Presence of Jesus in the Passage

What points to Jesus and His life in this passage? Does any verse remind you of something Jesus said or the way Jesus lived?

5. The Character of God

Who does God say that He is? Identify attributes from God's character in this passage. A good way to start, is to use words like: God is, God says, God does, God wants, or God can.
Review your previous answers.

6. The 'So What' or the Next Steps

Now, ask yourself, 'So what?' If what you read is true, how will you apply this? What will you do differently? What has to change?

7. Time to Pray

It is time to pray and ask God to help you. Write down your prayer to God based on what you are learning from today's passage and questions.

1. The Bible: Passage_____ and Date_____

_____/_____/_____

2. The New Thing

What is one new thing that stands out to you in today's passage?
It may be a verse you don't remember reading before.

3. The Wow Factor

What was the most important and impactful thing you read today? What made you say, "Wow! I'm blown away."

4. The Presence of Jesus in the Passage

What points to Jesus and His life in this passage? Does any verse remind you of something Jesus said or the way Jesus lived?

5. The Character of God

Who does God say that He is? Identify attributes from God's character in this passage. A good way to start, is to use words like: God is, God says, God does, God wants, or God can.
Review your previous answers.

6. The 'So What' or the Next Steps

Now, ask yourself, 'So what?' If what you read is true, how will you apply this? What will you do differently? What has to change?

7. Time to Pray

It is time to pray and ask God to help you. Write down your prayer to God based on what you are learning from today's passage and questions.

your **grace** *is* SUFFICIENT.

2 Corinthians 12:9

NEW TESTAMENT SOLUTION

```
M D 2 D M J D M U Y P H I L E M O N
Y A N H U Q E P 1 A J O H N P L P Y
H B T D C O A Y L C L E N N R B S
T J E T N O M I N K M H Q J H A T N
O S T V H O R L N V G Y B F O V A A
M U K L S E W I T H C H N O J X S I
I T P V W U W P N E N T E K Q N N N
T I Z W E E 2 P S T D O W L 3 G A O
B T R F R D A I S G H M L Z G U I L
2 K O Q B J J A E X P I J O H N S A
Q F M G E E O N M Q V T A Q Q C E S
R R A H H K H S A C X T U N I H H S
E E N F N U N G J A P 1 U F S B P E
T T S C O L O S S I A N S Y Q U E H
E E Y M W G R E V E L A T I O N X T
P P R 1 A C O R I N T H I A N S U X
S J 1 H T H E S S A L O N I A N S 2
1 2 M A R K P G A L A T I A N S R M
```

1. The Bible: Passage_____ and Date_____

_____/_____/_____

2. The New Thing

What is one new thing that stands out to you in today's passage?
It may be a verse you don't remember reading before.

3. The Wow Factor

What was the most important and impactful thing you read today? What made you say, "Wow! I'm blown away."

4. The Presence of Jesus in the Passage

What points to Jesus and His life in this passage? Does any verse remind you of something Jesus said or the way Jesus lived?

5. The Character of God

Who does God say that He is? Identify attributes from God's character in this passage. A good way to start, is to use words like: God is, God says, God does, God wants, or God can.
Review your previous answers.

6. The 'So What' or the Next Steps

Now, ask yourself, 'So what?' If what you read is true, how will you apply this? What will you do differently? What has to change?

7. Time to Pray

It is time to pray and ask God to help you. Write down your prayer to God based on what you are learning from today's passage and questions.

1. The Bible: Passage_____ and Date_____

_____/_____/_____

2. The New Thing

What is one new thing that stands out to you in today's passage?
It may be a verse you don't remember reading before.

3. The Wow Factor

What was the most important and impactful thing you read today? What made you say, "Wow! I'm blown away."

4. The Presence of Jesus in the Passage

What points to Jesus and His life in this passage? Does any verse remind you of something Jesus said or the way Jesus lived?

5. The Character of God

Who does God say that He is? Identify attributes from God's character in this passage. A good way to start, is to use words like: God is, God says, God does, God wants, or God can.
Review your previous answers.

6. The 'So What' or the Next Steps

Now, ask yourself, 'So what?' If what you read is true, how will you apply this? What will you do differently? What has to change?

7. Time to Pray

It is time to pray and ask God to help you. Write down your prayer to God based on what you are learning from today's passage and questions.

John 17:1–26

Jesus's prayer for His disciples

After saying all these things, Jesus looked up to heaven and said, "Father, the hour has come. Glorify your Son so he can give glory back to you. For you have given him authority over everyone. He gives eternal life to each one you have given him. And this is the way to have eternal life—to know you, the only true God, and Jesus Christ, the one you sent to earth. I brought glory to you here on earth by completing the work you gave me to do. Now, Father, bring me into the glory we shared before the world began. "I have revealed you[a] to the ones you gave me from this world. They were always yours. You gave them to me, and they have kept your word. Now they know that everything I have is a gift from you, for I have passed on to them the message you gave me. They accepted it and know that I came from you, and they believe you sent me. "My prayer is not for the world, but for those you have given me, because they belong to you. All who are mine belong to you, and you have given them to me, so they bring me glory. Now I am departing from the world; they are staying in this world, but I am coming to you. Holy Father, you have given me your name; now protect them by the power of your name so that they will be united just as we are. During my time here, I protected them by the power of the name you gave me. I guarded them so that not one was lost, except the one headed for destruction, as the Scriptures foretold. "Now I am coming to you. I told them many things while I was with them in this world so they would be filled with my joy. I have given them your word. And the world hates them because they do not belong to the world, just as I do not belong to the world. I'm not asking you to take them out of the world, but to keep them safe from the evil one. They do not belong to this world any more than I do. Make them holy by your truth; teach them your word, which is truth. Just as you sent me into the world, I am sending them into the world. And I give myself as a holy sacrifice for them so they can be made holy by your truth. "I am praying not only for these disciples but also for all who will ever believe in me through their message. I pray that they will all be one, just as you and I are one—as you are in me, Father, and I am in you. And may they be in us so that the world will believe you sent me. "I have given them the glory you gave me, so they may be one as we are one. I am in them and you are in me. May they experience such perfect unity that the world will know that you sent me and that you love them as much as you love me. Father, I want these whom you have given me to be with me where I am. Then they can see all the glory you gave me because you loved me even before the world began! "O righteous Father, the world doesn't know you, but I do; and these disciples know you sent me. I have revealed you to them, and I will continue to do so. Then your love for me will be in them, and I will be in them."

1. The Bible: Passage_____ and Date_____

_____/_____/_____

2. The New Thing

What is one new thing that stands out to you in today's passage?
It may be a verse you don't remember reading before.

3. The Wow Factor

What was the most important and impactful thing you read today? What made you say, "Wow! I'm blown away."

4. The Presence of Jesus in the Passage

What points to Jesus and His life in this passage? Does any verse remind you of something Jesus said or the way Jesus lived?

5. The Character of God

Who does God say that He is? Identify attributes from God's character in this passage. A good way to start, is to use words like: God is, God says, God does, God wants, or God can.
Review your previous answers.

6. The 'So What' or the Next Steps

Now, ask yourself, 'So what?' If what you read is true, how will you apply this? What will you do differently? What has to change?

7. Time to Pray

It is time to pray and ask God to help you. Write down your prayer to God based on what you are learning from today's passage and questions.

1. The Bible: Passage_____ and Date_____

_____/_____/_____

2. The New Thing

What is one new thing that stands out to you in today's passage?
It may be a verse you don't remember reading before.

3. The Wow Factor

What was the most important and impactful thing you read today? What made you say, "Wow! I'm blown away."

4. The Presence of Jesus in the Passage

What points to Jesus and His life in this passage? Does any verse remind you of something Jesus said or the way Jesus lived?

5. The Character of God

Who does God say that He is? Identify attributes from God's character in this passage. A good way to start, is to use words like: God is, God says, God does, God wants, or God can.
Review your previous answers.

6. The 'So What' or the Next Steps

Now, ask yourself, 'So what?' If what you read is true, how will you apply this? What will you do differently? What has to change?

7. Time to Pray

It is time to pray and ask God to help you. Write down your prayer to God based on what you are learning from today's passage and questions.

1. The Bible: Passage_____ and Date_____

_____/_____/_____

2. The New Thing

What is one new thing that stands out to you in today's passage?
It may be a verse you don't remember reading before.

3. The Wow Factor

What was the most important and impactful thing you read today? What made you say, "Wow! I'm blown away."

4. The Presence of Jesus in the Passage

What points to Jesus and His life in this passage? Does any verse remind you of something Jesus said or the way Jesus lived?

5. The Character of God

Who does God say that He is? Identify attributes from God's character in this passage. A good way to start, is to use words like: God is, God says, God does, God wants, or God can.
Review your previous answers.

6. The 'So What' or the Next Steps

Now, ask yourself, 'So what?' If what you read is true, how will you apply this? What will you do differently? What has to change?

7. Time to Pray

It is time to pray and ask God to help you. Write down your prayer to God based on what you are learning from today's passage and questions.

1 Samuel 2:1–10

Hannah's prayer

"My heart rejoices in the Lord! The Lord has made me strong. Now I have an answer for my enemies; I rejoice because you rescued me. No one is holy like the Lord! There is no one besides you; there is no Rock like our God. "Stop acting so proud and haughty! Don't speak with such arrogance! For the Lord is a God who knows what you have done; he will judge your actions. The bow of the mighty is now broken, and those who stumbled are now strong. Those who were well fed are now starving, and those who were starving are now full. The childless woman now has seven children, and the woman with many children wastes away. The Lord gives both death and life; he brings some down to the grave but raises others up. The Lord makes some poor and others rich; he brings some down and lifts others up. He lifts the poor from the dust and the needy from the garbage dump. He sets them among princes, placing them in seats of honor. For all the earth is the Lord's, and he has set the world in order. "He will protect his faithful ones, but the wicked will disappear in darkness. No one will succeed by strength alone. Those who fight against the Lord will be shattered. He thunders against them from heaven; the Lord judges throughout the earth. He gives power to his king; he increases the strength of his anointed one."

Prayers

1. The Bible: Passage_____ and Date_____

_____/_____/_____

2. The New Thing

What is one new thing that stands out to you in today's passage?
It may be a verse you don't remember reading before.

3. The Wow Factor

What was the most important and impactful thing you read today? What made you say, "Wow! I'm blown away."

4. The Presence of Jesus in the Passage

What points to Jesus and His life in this passage? Does any verse remind you of something Jesus said or the way Jesus lived?

5. The Character of God

Who does God say that He is? Identify attributes from God's character in this passage. A good way to start, is to use words like: God is, God says, God does, God wants, or God can.
Review your previous answers.

6. The 'So What' or the Next Steps

Now, ask yourself, 'So what?' If what you read is true, how will you apply this? What will you do differently? What has to change?

7. Time to Pray

It is time to pray and ask God to help you. Write down your prayer to God based on what you are learning from today's passage and questions.

1. The Bible: Passage_____ and Date_____

_____/_____/_____

2. The New Thing

What is one new thing that stands out to you in today's passage?
It may be a verse you don't remember reading before.

3. The Wow Factor

What was the most important and impactful thing you read today? What made you say, "Wow! I'm blown away."

4. The Presence of Jesus in the Passage

What points to Jesus and His life in this passage? Does any verse remind you of something Jesus said or the way Jesus lived?

5. The Character of God

Who does God say that He is? Identify attributes from God's character in this passage. A good way to start, is to use words like: God is, God says, God does, God wants, or God can.
Review your previous answers.

6. The 'So What' or the Next Steps

Now, ask yourself, 'So what?' If what you read is true, how will you apply this? What will you do differently? What has to change?

7. Time to Pray

It is time to pray and ask God to help you. Write down your prayer to God based on what you are learning from today's passage and questions.

1. The Bible: Passage_____ and Date_____

_____/_____/_____

2. The New Thing

What is one new thing that stands out to you in today's passage?
It may be a verse you don't remember reading before.

3. The Wow Factor

What was the most important and impactful thing you read today? What made you say, "Wow! I'm blown away."

4. The Presence of Jesus in the Passage

What points to Jesus and His life in this passage? Does any verse remind you of something Jesus said or the way Jesus lived?

BELIEVE
IT!

5. The Character of God

Who does God say that He is? Identify attributes from God's character in this passage. A good way to start, is to use words like: God is, God says, God does, God wants, or God can.
Review your previous answers.

6. The 'So What' or the Next Steps

Now, ask yourself, 'So what?' If what you read is true, how will you apply this? What will you do differently? What has to change?

7. Time to Pray

It is time to pray and ask God to help you. Write down your prayer to God based on what you are learning from today's passage and questions.

1. The Bible: Passage_____ and Date_____

_____/_____/_____

2. The New Thing

What is one new thing that stands out to you in today's passage?
It may be a verse you don't remember reading before.

3. The Wow Factor

What was the most important and impactful thing you read today? What made you say, "Wow! I'm blown away."

4. The Presence of Jesus in the Passage

What points to Jesus and His life in this passage? Does any verse remind you of something Jesus said or the way Jesus lived?

5. The Character of God

Who does God say that He is? Identify attributes from God's character in this passage. A good way to start, is to use words like: God is, God says, God does, God wants, or God can.
Review your previous answers.

6. The 'So What' or the Next Steps

Now, ask yourself, 'So what?' If what you read is true, how will you apply this? What will you do differently? What has to change?

7. Time to Pray

It is time to pray and ask God to help you. Write down your prayer to God based on what you are learning from today's passage and questions.

1. The Bible: Passage_____ and Date_____

_____/_____/_____

2. The New Thing

What is one new thing that stands out to you in today's passage?
It may be a verse you don't remember reading before.

3. The Wow Factor

What was the most important and impactful thing you read today? What made you say, "Wow! I'm blown away."

4. The Presence of Jesus in the Passage

What points to Jesus and His life in this passage? Does any verse remind you of something Jesus said or the way Jesus lived?

5. The Character of God

Who does God say that He is? Identify attributes from God's character in this passage. A good way to start, is to use words like: God is, God says, God does, God wants, or God can.
Review your previous answers.

6. The 'So What' or the Next Steps

Now, ask yourself, 'So what?' If what you read is true, how will you apply this? What will you do differently? What has to change?

7. Time to Pray

It is time to pray and ask God to help you. Write down your prayer to God based on what you are learning from today's passage and questions.

BEST PRAYERS

OF MY LIFE

fear Not
for I am
with you.
ISAIAH 58:11

1. The Bible: Passage_____ and Date_____

_____/_____/_____

2. The New Thing

What is one new thing that stands out to you in today's passage?
It may be a verse you don't remember reading before.

3. The Wow Factor

What was the most important and impactful thing you read today? What made you say, "Wow! I'm blown away."

4. The Presence of Jesus in the Passage

What points to Jesus and His life in this passage? Does any verse remind you of something Jesus said or the way Jesus lived?

5. The Character of God

Who does God say that He is? Identify attributes from God's character in this passage. A good way to start, is to use words like: God is, God says, God does, God wants, or God can.
Review your previous answers.

6. The 'So What' or the Next Steps

Now, ask yourself, 'So what?' If what you read is true, how will you apply this? What will you do differently? What has to change?

7. Time to Pray

It is time to pray and ask God to help you. Write down your prayer to God based on what you are learning from today's passage and questions.

1. The Bible: Passage_____ and Date_____

_____/_____/_____

2. The New Thing

What is one new thing that stands out to you in today's passage?
It may be a verse you don't remember reading before.

3. The Wow Factor

What was the most important and impactful thing you read today? What made you say, "Wow! I'm blown away."

4. The Presence of Jesus in the Passage

What points to Jesus and His life in this passage? Does any verse remind you of something Jesus said or the way Jesus lived?

5. The Character of God

Who does God say that He is? Identify attributes from God's character in this passage. A good way to start, is to use words like: God is, God says, God does, God wants, or God can.
Review your previous answers.

6. The 'So What' or the Next Steps

Now, ask yourself, 'So what?' If what you read is true, how will you apply this? What will you do differently? What has to change?

7. Time to Pray

It is time to pray and ask God to help you. Write down your prayer to God based on what you are learning from today's passage and questions.

1. The Bible: Passage_____ and Date_____

_____/_____/_____

2. The New Thing

What is one new thing that stands out to you in today's passage?
It may be a verse you don't remember reading before.

3. The Wow Factor

What was the most important and impactful thing you read today? What made you say, "Wow! I'm blown away."

4. The Presence of Jesus in the Passage

What points to Jesus and His life in this passage? Does any verse remind you of something Jesus said or the way Jesus lived?

5. The Character of God

Who does God say that He is? Identify attributes from God's character in this passage. A good way to start, is to use words like: God is, God says, God does, God wants, or God can.
Review your previous answers.

6. The 'So What' or the Next Steps

Now, ask yourself, 'So what?' If what you read is true, how will you apply this? What will you do differently? What has to change?

7. Time to Pray

It is time to pray and ask God to help you. Write down your prayer to God based on what you are learning from today's passage and questions.

1. The Bible: Passage_____ and Date_____

_____/_____/_____

2. The New Thing

What is one new thing that stands out to you in today's passage?
It may be a verse you don't remember reading before.

3. The Wow Factor

What was the most important and impactful thing you read today? What made you say, "Wow! I'm blown away."

4. The Presence of Jesus in the Passage

What points to Jesus and His life in this passage? Does any verse remind you of something Jesus said or the way Jesus lived?

5. The Character of God

Who does God say that He is? Identify attributes from God's character in this passage. A good way to start, is to use words like: God is, God says, God does, God wants, or God can.
Review your previous answers.

6. The 'So What' or the Next Steps

Now, ask yourself, 'So what?' If what you read is true, how will you apply this? What will you do differently? What has to change?

7. Time to Pray

It is time to pray and ask God to help you. Write down your prayer to God based on what you are learning from today's passage and questions.

1. The Bible: Passage_____ and Date_____

_____/_____/_____

2. The New Thing

What is one new thing that stands out to you in today's passage?
It may be a verse you don't remember reading before.

3. The Wow Factor

What was the most important and impactful thing you read today? What made you say, "Wow! I'm blown away."

4. The Presence of Jesus in the Passage

What points to Jesus and His life in this passage? Does any verse remind you of something Jesus said or the way Jesus lived?

5. The Character of God

Who does God say that He is? Identify attributes from God's character in this passage. A good way to start, is to use words like: God is, God says, God does, God wants, or God can.
Review your previous answers.

6. The 'So What' or the Next Steps

Now, ask yourself, 'So what?' If what you read is true, how will you apply this? What will you do differently? What has to change?

7. Time to Pray

It is time to pray and ask God to help you. Write down your prayer to God based on what you are learning from today's passage and questions.

BEST

PRAYERS

OF

MY

LIFE

I'm a whosoever.
JOHN 3:16

Psalms 51:1–13

Prayer for repentance

Have mercy on me, O God, because of your unfailing love. Because of your great compassion, blot out the stain of my sins. Wash me clean from my guilt. Purify me from my sin. For I recognize my rebellion; it haunts me day and night. Against you, and you alone, have I sinned; I have done what is evil in your sight. You will be proved right in what you say, and your judgment against me is just. For I was born a sinner—yes, from the moment my mother conceived me. But you desire honesty from the womb, teaching me wisdom even there. Purify me from my sins, and I will be clean; wash me, and I will be whiter than snow. Oh, give me back my joy again; you have broken me—now let me rejoice. Don't keep looking at my sins. Remove the stain of my guilt. Create in me a clean heart, O God. Renew a loyal spirit within me. Do not banish me from your presence, and don't take your Holy Spirit from me. Restore to me the joy of your salvation, and make me willing to obey you. Then I will teach your ways to rebels, and they will return to you.

1. The Bible: Passage_____ and Date_____

_____/_____/_____

2. The New Thing

What is one new thing that stands out to you in today's passage?
It may be a verse you don't remember reading before.

3. The Wow Factor

What was the most important and impactful thing you read today? What made you say, "Wow! I'm blown away."

4. The Presence of Jesus in the Passage

What points to Jesus and His life in this passage? Does any verse remind you of something Jesus said or the way Jesus lived?

5. The Character of God

Who does God say that He is? Identify attributes from God's character in this passage. A good way to start, is to use words like: God is, God says, God does, God wants, or God can.
Review your previous answers.

6. The 'So What' or the Next Steps

Now, ask yourself, 'So what?' If what you read is true, how will you apply this? What will you do differently? What has to change?

7. Time to Pray

It is time to pray and ask God to help you. Write down your prayer to God based on what you are learning from today's passage and questions.

1. The Bible: Passage_____ and Date_____

_____/_____/_____

2. The New Thing

What is one new thing that stands out to you in today's passage?
It may be a verse you don't remember reading before.

3. The Wow Factor

What was the most important and impactful thing you read today? What made you say, "Wow! I'm blown away."

4. The Presence of Jesus in the Passage

What points to Jesus and His life in this passage? Does any verse remind you of something Jesus said or the way Jesus lived?

5. The Character of God

Who does God say that He is? Identify attributes from God's character in this passage. A good way to start, is to use words like: God is, God says, God does, God wants, or God can.
Review your previous answers.

6. The 'So What' or the Next Steps

Now, ask yourself, 'So what?' If what you read is true, how will you apply this? What will you do differently? What has to change?

7. Time to Pray

It is time to pray and ask God to help you. Write down your prayer to God based on what you are learning from today's passage and questions.

1. The Bible: Passage_____ and Date_____

_____/_____/_____

2. The New Thing

What is one new thing that stands out to you in today's passage?
It may be a verse you don't remember reading before.

3. The Wow Factor

What was the most important and impactful thing you read today? What made you say, "Wow! I'm blown away."

4. The Presence of Jesus in the Passage

What points to Jesus and His life in this passage? Does any verse remind you of something Jesus said or the way Jesus lived?

5. The Character of God

Who does God say that He is? Identify attributes from God's character in this passage. A good way to start, is to use words like: God is, God says, God does, God wants, or God can.
Review your previous answers.

6. The 'So What' or the Next Steps

Now, ask yourself, 'So what?' If what you read is true, how will you apply this? What will you do differently? What has to change?

7. Time to Pray

It is time to pray and ask God to help you. Write down your prayer to God based on what you are learning from today's passage and questions.

1. The Bible: Passage_____ and Date_____

_____/_____/_____

2. The New Thing

What is one new thing that stands out to you in today's passage?
It may be a verse you don't remember reading before.

3. The Wow Factor

What was the most important and impactful thing you read today? What made you say, "Wow! I'm blown away."

4. The Presence of Jesus in the Passage

What points to Jesus and His life in this passage? Does any verse remind you of something Jesus said or the way Jesus lived?

5. The Character of God

Who does God say that He is? Identify attributes from God's character in this passage. A good way to start, is to use words like: God is, God says, God does, God wants, or God can.
Review your previous answers.

6. The 'So What' or the Next Steps

Now, ask yourself, 'So what?' If what you read is true, how will you apply this? What will you do differently? What has to change?

7. Time to Pray

It is time to pray and ask God to help you. Write down your prayer to God based on what you are learning from today's passage and questions.

1. The Bible: Passage_____ and Date_____

_____/_____/_____

2. The New Thing

What is one new thing that stands out to you in today's passage?
It may be a verse you don't remember reading before.

3. The Wow Factor

What was the most important and impactful thing you read today? What made you say, "Wow! I'm blown away."

4. The Presence of Jesus in the Passage

What points to Jesus and His life in this passage? Does any verse remind you of something Jesus said or the way Jesus lived?

5. The Character of God

Who does God say that He is? Identify attributes from God's character in this passage. A good way to start, is to use words like: God is, God says, God does, God wants, or God can.
Review your previous answers.

6. The 'So What' or the Next Steps

Now, ask yourself, 'So what?' If what you read is true, how will you apply this? What will you do differently? What has to change?

7. Time to Pray

It is time to pray and ask God to help you. Write down your prayer to God based on what you are learning from today's passage and questions.

OLD TESTAMENT

```
F W E D S R O Q Z Z P N N B V X O G
A S A Y E X O D U S V C D W J T B I
A H B R B J A C H R O N I C L E S F
O A T R Z J L C H H V E K I Y P O S
W I P G E E I G O T J H Q R R T A M
N A G E K V M Z S U O E X A B M C K
I S E Y V J O O E R B M M K U X N C
W I N J O E L R A K T I Z E F A H M
D J E I Y R S S P A Y A L U U U A S
T P S B B E E O M S D H H T I J N U
N X I Y Y M G O E L W O Y R L A O C
H Z S L Y I D S B Z A P S M E M J I
E A S B I A U R N A E S F G I O A T
E U N H W H J E O J D K P A N S D I
H H O A T B X B U F J I I L A I U V
W S X O Q G P M Q S Y O A A D D K E
J O W U T Y U U C D A Y L H L F Q L
F J I T Q Y E N E S T H E R Q E K B
```

GENESIS
EXODUS
LEVITICUS
NUMBERS
JOSHUA
JUDGES
RUTH
SAMUEL
KINGS
CHRONICLES
EZRA
NEHEMIAH
ESTHER
JOB
PSALMS
PROVERBS
ISAIAH
JEREMIAH
EZEKIAL

DANIEL   AMOS
HOSEA   OBADIAH
JOEL   JONAH

Prayers

1. The Bible: Passage_____ and Date_____

_____/_____/_____

2. The New Thing

What is one new thing that stands out to you in today's passage?
It may be a verse you don't remember reading before.

3. The Wow Factor

What was the most important and impactful thing you read today? What made you say, "Wow! I'm blown away."

4. The Presence of Jesus in the Passage

What points to Jesus and His life in this passage? Does any verse remind you of something Jesus said or the way Jesus lived?

5. The Character of God

Who does God say that He is? Identify attributes from God's character in this passage. A good way to start, is to use words like: God is, God says, God does, God wants, or God can.
Review your previous answers.

6. The 'So What' or the Next Steps

Now, ask yourself, 'So what?' If what you read is true, how will you apply this? What will you do differently? What has to change?

7. Time to Pray

It is time to pray and ask God to help you. Write down your prayer to God based on what you are learning from today's passage and questions.

1. The Bible: Passage_____ and Date_____

_____/_____/_____

2. The New Thing

What is one new thing that stands out to you in today's passage?
It may be a verse you don't remember reading before.

3. The Wow Factor

What was the most important and impactful thing you read today? What made you say, "Wow! I'm blown away."

4. The Presence of Jesus in the Passage

What points to Jesus and His life in this passage? Does any verse remind you of something Jesus said or the way Jesus lived?

5. The Character of God

Who does God say that He is? Identify attributes from God's character in this passage. A good way to start, is to use words like: God is, God says, God does, God wants, or God can.
Review your previous answers.

6. The 'So What' or the Next Steps

Now, ask yourself, 'So what?' If what you read is true, how will you apply this? What will you do differently? What has to change?

7. Time to Pray

It is time to pray and ask God to help you. Write down your prayer to God based on what you are learning from today's passage and questions.

1. The Bible: Passage_____ and Date_____

_____/_____/_____

2. The New Thing

What is one new thing that stands out to you in today's passage?
It may be a verse you don't remember reading before.

3. The Wow Factor

What was the most important and impactful thing you read today? What made you say, "Wow! I'm blown away."

4. The Presence of Jesus in the Passage

What points to Jesus and His life in this passage? Does any verse remind you of something Jesus said or the way Jesus lived?

5. The Character of God

Who does God say that He is? Identify attributes from God's character in this passage. A good way to start, is to use words like: God is, God says, God does, God wants, or God can.
Review your previous answers.

6. The 'So What' or the Next Steps

Now, ask yourself, 'So what?' If what you read is true, how will you apply this? What will you do differently? What has to change?

7. Time to Pray

It is time to pray and ask God to help you. Write down your prayer to God based on what you are learning from today's passage and questions.

1. The Bible: Passage_____ and Date_____

_____/_____/_____

2. The New Thing

What is one new thing that stands out to you in today's passage?
It may be a verse you don't remember reading before.

3. The Wow Factor

What was the most important and impactful thing you read today? What made you say, "Wow! I'm blown away."

4. The Presence of Jesus in the Passage

What points to Jesus and His life in this passage? Does any verse remind you of something Jesus said or the way Jesus lived?

5. The Character of God

Who does God say that He is? Identify attributes from God's character in this passage. A good way to start, is to use words like: God is, God says, God does, God wants, or God can.
Review your previous answers.

6. The 'So What' or the Next Steps

Now, ask yourself, 'So what?' If what you read is true, how will you apply this? What will you do differently? What has to change?

7. Time to Pray

It is time to pray and ask God to help you. Write down your prayer to God based on what you are learning from today's passage and questions.

1. The Bible: Passage_____ and Date_____

_____/_____/_____

2. The New Thing

What is one new thing that stands out to you in today's passage?
It may be a verse you don't remember reading before.

3. The Wow Factor

What was the most important and impactful thing you read today? What made you say, "Wow! I'm blown away."

4. The Presence of Jesus in the Passage

What points to Jesus and His life in this passage? Does any verse remind you of something Jesus said or the way Jesus lived?

5. The Character of God

Who does God say that He is? Identify attributes from God's character in this passage. A good way to start, is to use words like: God is, God says, God does, God wants, or God can.
Review your previous answers.

6. The 'So What' or the Next Steps

Now, ask yourself, 'So what?' If what you read is true, how will you apply this? What will you do differently? What has to change?

7. Time to Pray

It is time to pray and ask God to help you. Write down your prayer to God based on what you are learning from today's passage and questions.

Psalms 43

Prayer for help in trouble

Declare me innocent, O God! Defend me against these ungodly people. Rescue me from these unjust liars. For you are God, my only safe haven. Why have you tossed me aside?

Why must I wander around in grief, oppressed by my enemies? Send out your light and your truth; let them guide me. Let them lead me to your holy mountain, to the place where you live. There I will go to the altar of God, to God—the source of all my joy. I will praise you with my harp, O God, my God! Why am I discouraged? Why is my heart so sad? I will put my hope in God! I will praise him again—my Savior and my God!

Prayers

1. The Bible: Passage_____ and Date_____

_____/_____/_____

2. The New Thing

What is one new thing that stands out to you in today's passage?
It may be a verse you don't remember reading before.

3. The Wow Factor

What was the most important and impactful thing you read today? What made you say, "Wow! I'm blown away."

4. The Presence of Jesus in the Passage

What points to Jesus and His life in this passage? Does any verse remind you of something Jesus said or the way Jesus lived?

5. The Character of God

Who does God say that He is? Identify attributes from God's character in this passage. A good way to start, is to use words like: God is, God says, God does, God wants, or God can.
Review your previous answers.

6. The 'So What' or the Next Steps

Now, ask yourself, 'So what?' If what you read is true, how will you apply this? What will you do differently? What has to change?

7. Time to Pray

It is time to pray and ask God to help you. Write down your prayer to God based on what you are learning from today's passage and questions.

1. The Bible: Passage_____ and Date_____

_____/_____/_____

2. The New Thing

What is one new thing that stands out to you in today's passage?
It may be a verse you don't remember reading before.

3. The Wow Factor

What was the most important and impactful thing you read today? What made you say, "Wow! I'm blown away."

4. The Presence of Jesus in the Passage

What points to Jesus and His life in this passage? Does any verse remind you of something Jesus said or the way Jesus lived?

5. The Character of God

Who does God say that He is? Identify attributes from God's character in this passage. A good way to start, is to use words like: God is, God says, God does, God wants, or God can.
Review your previous answers.

6. The 'So What' or the Next Steps

Now, ask yourself, 'So what?' If what you read is true, how will you apply this? What will you do differently? What has to change?

7. Time to Pray

It is time to pray and ask God to help you. Write down your prayer to God based on what you are learning from today's passage and questions.

1. The Bible: Passage_____ and Date_____

_____/_____/_____

2. The New Thing

What is one new thing that stands out to you in today's passage?
It may be a verse you don't remember reading before.

3. The Wow Factor

What was the most important and impactful thing you read today? What made you say, "Wow! I'm blown away."

4. The Presence of Jesus in the Passage

What points to Jesus and His life in this passage? Does any verse remind you of something Jesus said or the way Jesus lived?

5. The Character of God

Who does God say that He is? Identify attributes from God's character in this passage. A good way to start, is to use words like: God is, God says, God does, God wants, or God can.
Review your previous answers.

6. The 'So What' or the Next Steps

Now, ask yourself, 'So what?' If what you read is true, how will you apply this? What will you do differently? What has to change?

7. Time to Pray

It is time to pray and ask God to help you. Write down your prayer to God based on what you are learning from today's passage and questions.

1. The Bible: Passage_____ and Date_____

_____/_____/_____

2. The New Thing

What is one new thing that stands out to you in today's passage?
It may be a verse you don't remember reading before.

3. The Wow Factor

What was the most important and impactful thing you read today? What made you say, "Wow! I'm blown away."

4. The Presence of Jesus in the Passage

What points to Jesus and His life in this passage? Does any verse remind you of something Jesus said or the way Jesus lived?

5. The Character of God

Who does God say that He is? Identify attributes from God's character in this passage. A good way to start, is to use words like: God is, God says, God does, God wants, or God can.
Review your previous answers.

6. The 'So What' or the Next Steps

Now, ask yourself, 'So what?' If what you read is true, how will you apply this? What will you do differently? What has to change?

7. Time to Pray

It is time to pray and ask God to help you. Write down your prayer to God based on what you are learning from today's passage and questions.

1. The Bible: Passage_____ and Date_____

_____/_____/_____

2. The New Thing

What is one new thing that stands out to you in today's passage?
It may be a verse you don't remember reading before.

3. The Wow Factor

What was the most important and impactful thing you read today? What made you say, "Wow! I'm blown away."

4. The Presence of Jesus in the Passage

What points to Jesus and His life in this passage? Does any verse remind you of something Jesus said or the way Jesus lived?

5. The Character of God

Who does God say that He is? Identify attributes from God's character in this passage. A good way to start, is to use words like: God is, God says, God does, God wants, or God can.
Review your previous answers.

6. The 'So What' or the Next Steps

Now, ask yourself, 'So what?' If what you read is true, how will you apply this? What will you do differently? What has to change?

7. Time to Pray

It is time to pray and ask God to help you. Write down your prayer to God based on what you are learning from today's passage and questions.

BEST
PRAYERS

OF MY
LIFE

My CUP
runneth
OVER
Psalm 23:5

1. The Bible: Passage_____ and Date_____

_____/_____/_____

2. The New Thing

What is one new thing that stands out to you in today's passage?
It may be a verse you don't remember reading before.

3. The Wow Factor

What was the most important and impactful thing you read today? What made you say, "Wow! I'm blown away."

4. The Presence of Jesus in the Passage

What points to Jesus and His life in this passage? Does any verse remind you of something Jesus said or the way Jesus lived?

5. The Character of God

Who does God say that He is? Identify attributes from God's character in this passage. A good way to start, is to use words like: God is, God says, God does, God wants, or God can.
Review your previous answers.

6. The 'So What' or the Next Steps

Now, ask yourself, 'So what?' If what you read is true, how will you apply this? What will you do differently? What has to change?

7. Time to Pray

It is time to pray and ask God to help you. Write down your prayer to God based on what you are learning from today's passage and questions.

1. The Bible: Passage_____ and Date_____

_____/_____/_____

2. The New Thing

What is one new thing that stands out to you in today's passage?
It may be a verse you don't remember reading before.

3. The Wow Factor

What was the most important and impactful thing you read today? What made you say, "Wow! I'm blown away."

4. The Presence of Jesus in the Passage

What points to Jesus and His life in this passage? Does any verse remind you of something Jesus said or the way Jesus lived?

5. The Character of God

Who does God say that He is? Identify attributes from God's character in this passage. A good way to start, is to use words like: God is, God says, God does, God wants, or God can.
Review your previous answers.

6. The 'So What' or the Next Steps

Now, ask yourself, 'So what?' If what you read is true, how will you apply this? What will you do differently? What has to change?

7. Time to Pray

It is time to pray and ask God to help you. Write down your prayer to God based on what you are learning from today's passage and questions.

1. The Bible: Passage_____ and Date_____

_____/_____/_____

2. The New Thing

What is one new thing that stands out to you in today's passage?
It may be a verse you don't remember reading before.

3. The Wow Factor

What was the most important and impactful thing you read today? What made you say, "Wow! I'm blown away."

4. The Presence of Jesus in the Passage

What points to Jesus and His life in this passage? Does any verse remind you of something Jesus said or the way Jesus lived?

BELIEVE IT!

5. The Character of God

Who does God say that He is? Identify attributes from God's character in this passage. A good way to start, is to use words like: God is, God says, God does, God wants, or God can.
Review your previous answers.

6. The 'So What' or the Next Steps

Now, ask yourself, 'So what?' If what you read is true, how will you apply this? What will you do differently? What has to change?

7. Time to Pray

It is time to pray and ask God to help you. Write down your prayer to God based on what you are learning from today's passage and questions.

1. The Bible: Passage_____ and Date_____

_____/_____/_____

2. The New Thing

What is one new thing that stands out to you in today's passage?
It may be a verse you don't remember reading before.

3. The Wow Factor

What was the most important and impactful thing you read today? What made you say, "Wow! I'm blown away."

4. The Presence of Jesus in the Passage

What points to Jesus and His life in this passage? Does any verse remind you of something Jesus said or the way Jesus lived?

5. The Character of God

Who does God say that He is? Identify attributes from God's character in this passage. A good way to start, is to use words like: God is, God says, God does, God wants, or God can.
Review your previous answers.

6. The 'So What' or the Next Steps

Now, ask yourself, 'So what?' If what you read is true, how will you apply this? What will you do differently? What has to change?

7. Time to Pray

It is time to pray and ask God to help you. Write down your prayer to God based on what you are learning from today's passage and questions.

1. The Bible: Passage_____ and Date_____

_____/_____/_____

2. The New Thing

What is one new thing that stands out to you in today's passage?
It may be a verse you don't remember reading before.

3. The Wow Factor

What was the most important and impactful thing you read today? What made you say, "Wow! I'm blown away."

4. The Presence of Jesus in the Passage

What points to Jesus and His life in this passage? Does any verse remind you of something Jesus said or the way Jesus lived?

5. The Character of God

Who does God say that He is? Identify attributes from God's character in this passage. A good way to start, is to use words like: God is, God says, God does, God wants, or God can.
Review your previous answers.

6. The 'So What' or the Next Steps

Now, ask yourself, 'So what?' If what you read is true, how will you apply this? What will you do differently? What has to change?

7. Time to Pray

It is time to pray and ask God to help you. Write down your prayer to God based on what you are learning from today's passage and questions.

BEST PRAYERS

OF MY LIFE

Psalms 57

Prayer for safety from enemies

Have mercy on me, O God, have mercy! I look to you for protection. I will hide beneath the shadow of your wings until the danger passes by. I cry out to God Most High, to God who will fulfill his purpose for me. He will send help from heaven to rescue me, disgracing those who hound me. My God will send forth his unfailing love and faithfulness. I am surrounded by fierce lions who greedily devour human prey—
whose teeth pierce like spears and arrows, and whose tongues cut like swords. Be exalted, O God, above the highest heavens! May your glory shine over all the earth. My enemies have set a trap for me. I am weary from distress. They have dug a deep pit in my path, but they themselves have fallen into it. My heart is confident in you, O God; my heart is confident. No wonder I can sing your praises! Wake up, my heart! Wake up, O lyre and harp! I will wake the dawn with my song. I will thank you, Lord, among all the people. I will sing your praises among the nations. For your unfailing love is as high as the heavens. Your faithfulness reaches to the clouds. Be exalted, O God, above the highest heavens. May your glory shine over all the earth.

Walk BY faith

2 Corinthians 5:7

1. The Bible: Passage_____ and Date_____

_____/_____/_____

2. The New Thing

What is one new thing that stands out to you in today's passage?
It may be a verse you don't remember reading before.

3. The Wow Factor

What was the most important and impactful thing you read today? What made you say, "Wow! I'm blown away."

4. The Presence of Jesus in the Passage

What points to Jesus and His life in this passage? Does any verse remind you of something Jesus said or the way Jesus lived?

5. The Character of God

Who does God say that He is? Identify attributes from God's character in this passage. A good way to start, is to use words like: God is, God says, God does, God wants, or God can.
Review your previous answers.

6. The 'So What' or the Next Steps

Now, ask yourself, 'So what?' If what you read is true, how will you apply this? What will you do differently? What has to change?

7. Time to Pray

It is time to pray and ask God to help you. Write down your prayer to God based on what you are learning from today's passage and questions.

1. The Bible: Passage_____ and Date_____

_____/_____/_____

2. The New Thing

What is one new thing that stands out to you in today's passage?
It may be a verse you don't remember reading before.

3. The Wow Factor

What was the most important and impactful thing you read today? What made you say, "Wow! I'm blown away."

4. The Presence of Jesus in the Passage

What points to Jesus and His life in this passage? Does any verse remind you of something Jesus said or the way Jesus lived?

5. The Character of God

Who does God say that He is? Identify attributes from God's character in this passage. A good way to start, is to use words like: God is, God says, God does, God wants, or God can.
Review your previous answers.

6. The 'So What' or the Next Steps

Now, ask yourself, 'So what?' If what you read is true, how will you apply this? What will you do differently? What has to change?

7. Time to Pray

It is time to pray and ask God to help you. Write down your prayer to God based on what you are learning from today's passage and questions.

1. The Bible: Passage_____ and Date_____

_____/_____/_____

2. The New Thing

What is one new thing that stands out to you in today's passage?
It may be a verse you don't remember reading before.

3. The Wow Factor

What was the most important and impactful thing you read today? What made you say, "Wow! I'm blown away."

4. The Presence of Jesus in the Passage

What points to Jesus and His life in this passage? Does any verse remind you of something Jesus said or the way Jesus lived?

5. The Character of God

Who does God say that He is? Identify attributes from God's character in this passage. A good way to start, is to use words like: God is, God says, God does, God wants, or God can.
Review your previous answers.

6. The 'So What' or the Next Steps

Now, ask yourself, 'So what?' If what you read is true, how will you apply this? What will you do differently? What has to change?

7. Time to Pray

It is time to pray and ask God to help you. Write down your prayer to God based on what you are learning from today's passage and questions.

1. The Bible: Passage_____ and Date_____

_____/_____/_____

2. The New Thing

What is one new thing that stands out to you in today's passage?
It may be a verse you don't remember reading before.

3. The Wow Factor

What was the most important and impactful thing you read today? What made you say, "Wow! I'm blown away."

4. The Presence of Jesus in the Passage

What points to Jesus and His life in this passage? Does any verse remind you of something Jesus said or the way Jesus lived?

5. The Character of God

Who does God say that He is? Identify attributes from God's character in this passage. A good way to start, is to use words like: God is, God says, God does, God wants, or God can.
Review your previous answers.

6. The 'So What' or the Next Steps

Now, ask yourself, 'So what?' If what you read is true, how will you apply this? What will you do differently? What has to change?

7. Time to Pray

It is time to pray and ask God to help you. Write down your prayer to God based on what you are learning from today's passage and questions.

1. The Bible: Passage_____ and Date_____

_____/_____/_____

2. The New Thing

What is one new thing that stands out to you in today's passage?
It may be a verse you don't remember reading before.

3. The Wow Factor

What was the most important and impactful thing you read today? What made you say, "Wow! I'm blown away."

4. The Presence of Jesus in the Passage

What points to Jesus and His life in this passage? Does any verse remind you of something Jesus said or the way Jesus lived?

5. The Character of God

Who does God say that He is? Identify attributes from God's character in this passage. A good way to start, is to use words like: God is, God says, God does, God wants, or God can.
Review your previous answers.

6. The 'So What' or the Next Steps

Now, ask yourself, 'So what?' If what you read is true, how will you apply this? What will you do differently? What has to change?

7. Time to Pray

It is time to pray and ask God to help you. Write down your prayer to God based on what you are learning from today's passage and questions.

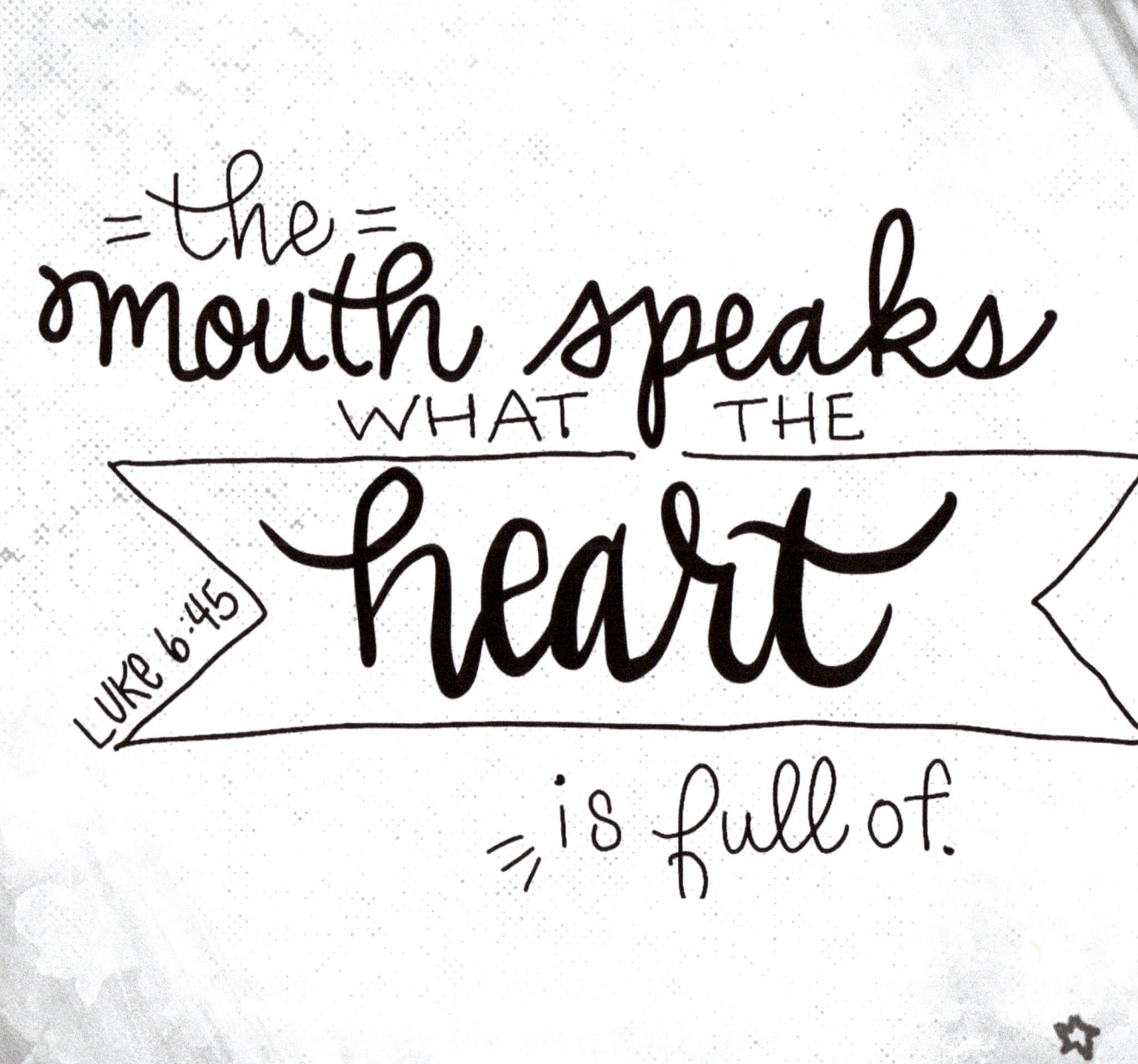

the mouth speaks what the heart is full of.

Luke 6:45

Prayers

1. The Bible: Passage_____ and Date_____

_____/_____/_____

2. The New Thing

What is one new thing that stands out to you in today's passage?
It may be a verse you don't remember reading before.

3. The Wow Factor

What was the most important and impactful thing you read today? What made you say, "Wow! I'm blown away."

4. The Presence of Jesus in the Passage

What points to Jesus and His life in this passage? Does any verse remind you of something Jesus said or the way Jesus lived?

5. The Character of God

Who does God say that He is? Identify attributes from God's character in this passage. A good way to start, is to use words like: God is, God says, God does, God wants, or God can.
Review your previous answers.

6. The 'So What' or the Next Steps

Now, ask yourself, 'So what?' If what you read is true, how will you apply this? What will you do differently? What has to change?

7. Time to Pray

It is time to pray and ask God to help you. Write down your prayer to God based on what you are learning from today's passage and questions.

1. The Bible: Passage_____ and Date_____

_____/_____/_____

2. The New Thing

What is one new thing that stands out to you in today's passage?
It may be a verse you don't remember reading before.

3. The Wow Factor

What was the most important and impactful thing you read today? What made you say, "Wow! I'm blown away."

4. The Presence of Jesus in the Passage

What points to Jesus and His life in this passage? Does any verse remind you of something Jesus said or the way Jesus lived?

5. The Character of God

Who does God say that He is? Identify attributes from God's character in this passage. A good way to start, is to use words like: God is, God says, God does, God wants, or God can.
Review your previous answers.

6. The 'So What' or the Next Steps

Now, ask yourself, 'So what?' If what you read is true, how will you apply this? What will you do differently? What has to change?

7. Time to Pray

It is time to pray and ask God to help you. Write down your prayer to God based on what you are learning from today's passage and questions.

1. The Bible: Passage_____ and Date_____

_____/_____/_____

2. The New Thing

What is one new thing that stands out to you in today's passage?
It may be a verse you don't remember reading before.

3. The Wow Factor

What was the most important and impactful thing you read today? What made you say, "Wow! I'm blown away."

4. The Presence of Jesus in the Passage

What points to Jesus and His life in this passage? Does any verse remind you of something Jesus said or the way Jesus lived?

5. The Character of God

Who does God say that He is? Identify attributes from God's character in this passage. A good way to start, is to use words like: God is, God says, God does, God wants, or God can.
Review your previous answers.

6. The 'So What' or the Next Steps

Now, ask yourself, 'So what?' If what you read is true, how will you apply this? What will you do differently? What has to change?

7. Time to Pray

It is time to pray and ask God to help you. Write down your prayer to God based on what you are learning from today's passage and questions.

1. The Bible: Passage_____ and Date_____

_____/_____/_____

2. The New Thing

What is one new thing that stands out to you in today's passage?
It may be a verse you don't remember reading before.

3. The Wow Factor

What was the most important and impactful thing you read today? What made you say, "Wow! I'm blown away."

4. The Presence of Jesus in the Passage

What points to Jesus and His life in this passage? Does any verse remind you of something Jesus said or the way Jesus lived?

5. The Character of God

Who does God say that He is? Identify attributes from God's character in this passage. A good way to start, is to use words like: God is, God says, God does, God wants, or God can.
Review your previous answers.

6. The 'So What' or the Next Steps

Now, ask yourself, 'So what?' If what you read is true, how will you apply this? What will you do differently? What has to change?

7. Time to Pray

It is time to pray and ask God to help you. Write down your prayer to God based on what you are learning from today's passage and questions.

1. The Bible: Passage_____ and Date_____

_____/_____/_____

2. The New Thing

What is one new thing that stands out to you in today's passage?
It may be a verse you don't remember reading before.

3. The Wow Factor

What was the most important and impactful thing you read today? What made you say, "Wow! I'm blown away."

4. The Presence of Jesus in the Passage

What points to Jesus and His life in this passage? Does any verse remind you of something Jesus said or the way Jesus lived?

5. The Character of God

Who does God say that He is? Identify attributes from God's character in this passage. A good way to start, is to use words like: God is, God says, God does, God wants, or God can.
Review your previous answers.

6. The 'So What' or the Next Steps

Now, ask yourself, 'So what?' If what you read is true, how will you apply this? What will you do differently? What has to change?

7. Time to Pray

It is time to pray and ask God to help you. Write down your prayer to God based on what you are learning from today's passage and questions.

BEST
PRAYERS

OF
MY

LIFE

OLD TESTAMENT SOLUTION

```
F W E D S R O Q Z Z P N N B V X O G
A S A Y E X O D U S V C D W J T B I
A H B R B J A C H R O N I C L E S F
O A T R Z J L C H H V E K I Y P O S
W I P G E E I G O T J H Q R R T A M
N A G E K V M Z S U O E X A B M C K
I S E Y V J O O E R B M M K U X N C
W I N J O E L R A K T I Z E F A H M
D J E I Y R S S P A Y A L U U U A S
T P S B B E E O M S D H H T I J N U
N X I Y Y M G O E L W O Y R L A O C
H Z S L Y I D S B Z A P S M E M J I
E A S B I A U R N A E S F G I O A T
E U N H W H J E O J D K P A N S D I
H H O A T B X B U F J I L A I U V
W S X O Q G P M Q S Y O A A D D K E
J O W U T Y U U C D A Y L H L F Q L
F J I T Q Y E N E S T H E R Q E K B
```

1. The Bible: Passage_____ and Date_____

_____/_____/_____

2. The New Thing

What is one new thing that stands out to you in today's passage?
It may be a verse you don't remember reading before.

3. The Wow Factor

What was the most important and impactful thing you read today? What made you say, "Wow! I'm blown away."

4. The Presence of Jesus in the Passage

What points to Jesus and His life in this passage? Does any verse remind you of something Jesus said or the way Jesus lived?

5. The Character of God

Who does God say that He is? Identify attributes from God's character in this passage. A good way to start, is to use words like: God is, God says, God does, God wants, or God can.
Review your previous answers.

6. The 'So What' or the Next Steps

Now, ask yourself, 'So what?' If what you read is true, how will you apply this? What will you do differently? What has to change?

7. Time to Pray

It is time to pray and ask God to help you. Write down your prayer to God based on what you are learning from today's passage and questions.

1. The Bible: Passage_____ and Date_____

_____/_____/_____

2. The New Thing

What is one new thing that stands out to you in today's passage?
It may be a verse you don't remember reading before.

3. The Wow Factor

What was the most important and impactful thing you read today? What made you say, "Wow! I'm blown away."

4. The Presence of Jesus in the Passage

What points to Jesus and His life in this passage? Does any verse remind you of something Jesus said or the way Jesus lived?

5. The Character of God

Who does God say that He is? Identify attributes from God's character in this passage. A good way to start, is to use words like: God is, God says, God does, God wants, or God can.
Review your previous answers.

6. The 'So What' or the Next Steps

Now, ask yourself, 'So what?' If what you read is true, how will you apply this? What will you do differently? What has to change?

7. Time to Pray

It is time to pray and ask God to help you. Write down your prayer to God based on what you are learning from today's passage and questions.

1. The Bible: Passage_____ and Date_____

_____/_____/_____

2. The New Thing

What is one new thing that stands out to you in today's passage?
It may be a verse you don't remember reading before.

3. The Wow Factor

What was the most important and impactful thing you read today? What made you say, "Wow! I'm blown away."

4. The Presence of Jesus in the Passage

What points to Jesus and His life in this passage? Does any verse remind you of something Jesus said or the way Jesus lived?

5. The Character of God

Who does God say that He is? Identify attributes from God's character in this passage. A good way to start, is to use words like: God is, God says, God does, God wants, or God can.
Review your previous answers.

6. The 'So What' or the Next Steps

Now, ask yourself, 'So what?' If what you read is true, how will you apply this? What will you do differently? What has to change?

7. Time to Pray

It is time to pray and ask God to help you. Write down your prayer to God based on what you are learning from today's passage and questions.

1. The Bible: Passage_____ and Date_____

_____/_____/_____

2. The New Thing

What is one new thing that stands out to you in today's passage?
It may be a verse you don't remember reading before.

3. The Wow Factor

What was the most important and impactful thing you read today? What made you say, "Wow! I'm blown away."

4. The Presence of Jesus in the Passage

What points to Jesus and His life in this passage? Does any verse remind you of something Jesus said or the way Jesus lived?

5. The Character of God

Who does God say that He is? Identify attributes from God's character in this passage. A good way to start, is to use words like: God is, God says, God does, God wants, or God can.
Review your previous answers.

6. The 'So What' or the Next Steps

Now, ask yourself, 'So what?' If what you read is true, how will you apply this? What will you do differently? What has to change?

7. Time to Pray

It is time to pray and ask God to help you. Write down your prayer to God based on what you are learning from today's passage and questions.

1. The Bible: Passage_____ and Date_____

_____/_____/_____

2. The New Thing

What is one new thing that stands out to you in today's passage?
It may be a verse you don't remember reading before.

3. The Wow Factor

What was the most important and impactful thing you read today? What made you say, "Wow! I'm blown away."

4. The Presence of Jesus in the Passage

What points to Jesus and His life in this passage? Does any verse remind you of something Jesus said or the way Jesus lived?

5. The Character of God

Who does God say that He is? Identify attributes from God's character in this passage. A good way to start, is to use words like: God is, God says, God does, God wants, or God can.
Review your previous answers.

6. The 'So What' or the Next Steps

Now, ask yourself, 'So what?' If what you read is true, how will you apply this? What will you do differently? What has to change?

7. Time to Pray

It is time to pray and ask God to help you. Write down your prayer to God based on what you are learning from today's passage and questions.

Psalms 86

Prayer for mercy

Bend down, O LORD, and hear my prayer; answer me, for I need your help. Protect me, for I am devoted to you. Save me, for I serve you and trust you. You are my God. Be merciful to me, O Lord, for I am calling on you constantly. Give me happiness, O Lord, for I give myself to you. O Lord, you are so good, so ready to forgive, so full of unfailing love for all who ask for your help. Listen closely to my prayer, O LORD; hear my urgent cry. I will call to you whenever I'm in trouble, and you will answer me. No pagan god is like you, O Lord. None can do what you do! All the nations you made will come and bow before you, Lord; they will praise your holy name. For you are great and perform wonderful deeds. You alone are God. Teach your ways, O LORD, that I may live according to your truth! Grant me purity of heart, so that I may honor you. With all my heart I will praise you, O Lord my God. I will give glory to your name forever, for your love for me is very great. You have rescued me from the depths of death. O God, insolent people rise up against me; a violent gang is trying to kill me. You mean nothing to them. But you, O Lord, are a God of compassion and mercy, slow to get angry and filled with unfailing love and faithfulness. Look down and have mercy on me. Give your strength to your servant; save me, the son of your servant. Send me a sign of your favor. Then those who hate me will be put to shame, for you, O LORD, help and comfort me.

Prayers

1. The Bible: Passage_____ and Date_____

_____/_____/_____

2. The New Thing

What is one new thing that stands out to you in today's passage?
It may be a verse you don't remember reading before.

3. The Wow Factor

What was the most important and impactful thing you read today? What made you say, "Wow! I'm blown away."

4. The Presence of Jesus in the Passage

What points to Jesus and His life in this passage? Does any verse remind you of something Jesus said or the way Jesus lived?

5. The Character of God

Who does God say that He is? Identify attributes from God's character in this passage. A good way to start, is to use words like: God is, God says, God does, God wants, or God can.
Review your previous answers.

6. The 'So What' or the Next Steps

Now, ask yourself, 'So what?' If what you read is true, how will you apply this? What will you do differently? What has to change?

7. Time to Pray

It is time to pray and ask God to help you. Write down your prayer to God based on what you are learning from today's passage and questions.

1. The Bible: Passage_____ and Date_____

_____/_____/_____

2. The New Thing

What is one new thing that stands out to you in today's passage?
It may be a verse you don't remember reading before.

3. The Wow Factor

What was the most important and impactful thing you read today? What made you say, "Wow! I'm blown away."

4. The Presence of Jesus in the Passage

What points to Jesus and His life in this passage? Does any verse remind you of something Jesus said or the way Jesus lived?

5. The Character of God

Who does God say that He is? Identify attributes from God's character in this passage. A good way to start, is to use words like: God is, God says, God does, God wants, or God can.
Review your previous answers.

6. The 'So What' or the Next Steps

Now, ask yourself, 'So what?' If what you read is true, how will you apply this? What will you do differently? What has to change?

7. Time to Pray

It is time to pray and ask God to help you. Write down your prayer to God based on what you are learning from today's passage and questions.

1. The Bible: Passage_____ and Date_____

_____/_____/_____

2. The New Thing

What is one new thing that stands out to you in today's passage?
It may be a verse you don't remember reading before.

3. The Wow Factor

What was the most important and impactful thing you read today? What made you say, "Wow! I'm blown away."

4. The Presence of Jesus in the Passage

What points to Jesus and His life in this passage? Does any verse remind you of something Jesus said or the way Jesus lived?

5. The Character of God

Who does God say that He is? Identify attributes from God's character in this passage. A good way to start, is to use words like: God is, God says, God does, God wants, or God can.
Review your previous answers.

6. The 'So What' or the Next Steps

Now, ask yourself, 'So what?' If what you read is true, how will you apply this? What will you do differently? What has to change?

7. Time to Pray

It is time to pray and ask God to help you. Write down your prayer to God based on what you are learning from today's passage and questions.

1. The Bible: Passage_____ and Date_____

_____/_____/_____

2. The New Thing

What is one new thing that stands out to you in today's passage?
It may be a verse you don't remember reading before.

3. The Wow Factor

What was the most important and impactful thing you read today? What made you say, "Wow! I'm
blown away."

4. The Presence of Jesus in the Passage

What points to Jesus and His life in this passage? Does any verse remind you of something Jesus said
or the way Jesus lived?

5. The Character of God

Who does God say that He is? Identify attributes from God's character in this passage. A good way to start, is to use words like: God is, God says, God does, God wants, or God can.
Review your previous answers.

6. The 'So What' or the Next Steps

Now, ask yourself, 'So what?' If what you read is true, how will you apply this? What will you do differently? What has to change?

7. Time to Pray

It is time to pray and ask God to help you. Write down your prayer to God based on what you are learning from today's passage and questions.

1. The Bible: Passage_____ and Date_____

_____/_____/_____

2. The New Thing

What is one new thing that stands out to you in today's passage?
It may be a verse you don't remember reading before.

3. The Wow Factor

What was the most important and impactful thing you read today? What made you say, "Wow! I'm blown away."

4. The Presence of Jesus in the Passage

What points to Jesus and His life in this passage? Does any verse remind you of something Jesus said or the way Jesus lived?

5. The Character of God

Who does God say that He is? Identify attributes from God's character in this passage. A good way to start, is to use words like: God is, God says, God does, God wants, or God can.
Review your previous answers.

6. The 'So What' or the Next Steps

Now, ask yourself, 'So what?' If what you read is true, how will you apply this? What will you do differently? What has to change?

7. Time to Pray

It is time to pray and ask God to help you. Write down your prayer to God based on what you are learning from today's passage and questions.

BEST
PRAYERS

OF
MY
LIFE

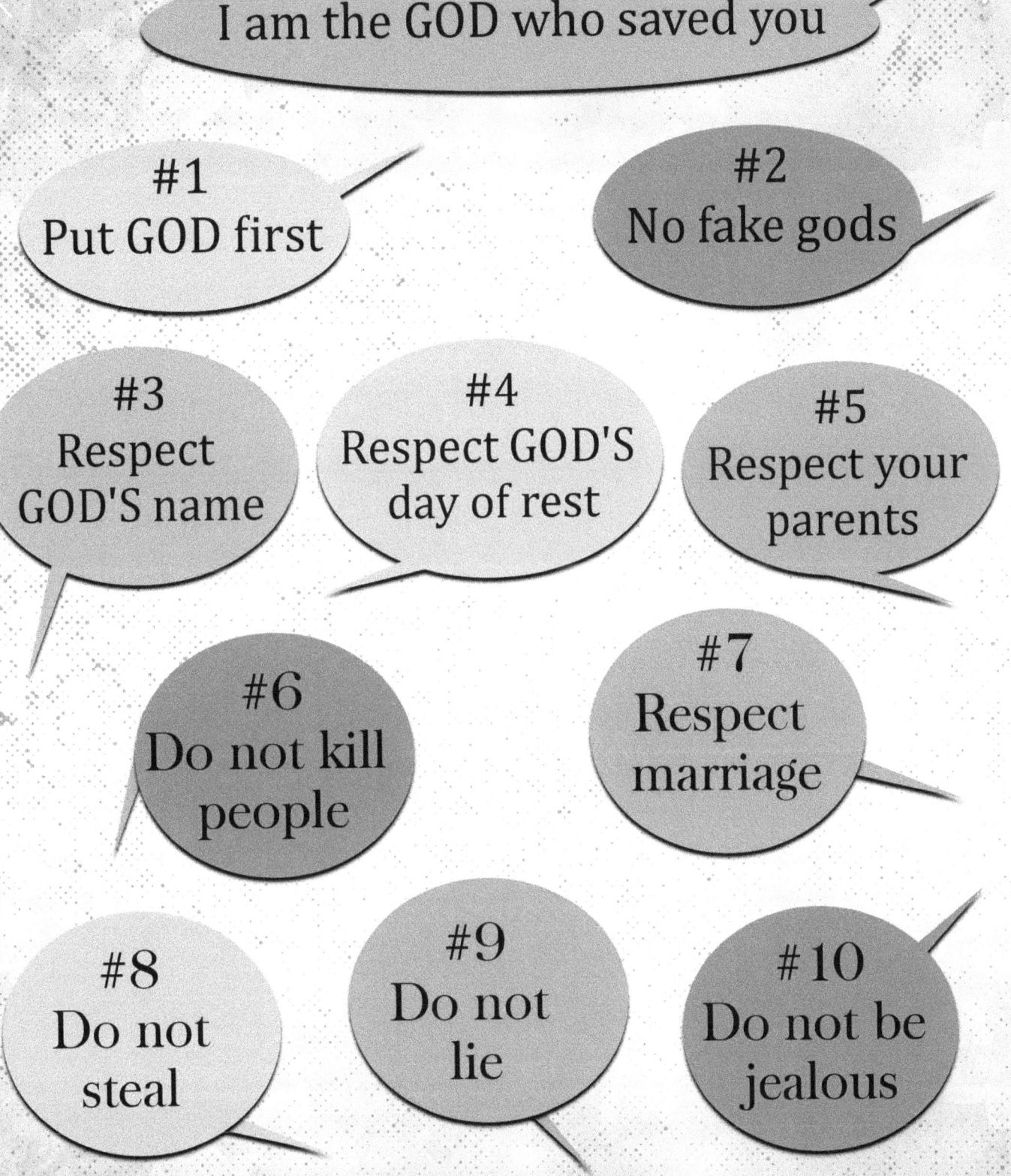

THE 10 COMMANDMENTS
{Exodus 20:2-17 paraphrase}

1. The Bible: Passage_____ and Date_____

_____/_____/_____

2. The New Thing

What is one new thing that stands out to you in today's passage?
It may be a verse you don't remember reading before.

3. The Wow Factor

What was the most important and impactful thing you read today? What made you say, "Wow! I'm blown away."

4. The Presence of Jesus in the Passage

What points to Jesus and His life in this passage? Does any verse remind you of something Jesus said or the way Jesus lived?

5. The Character of God

Who does God say that He is? Identify attributes from God's character in this passage. A good way to start, is to use words like: God is, God says, God does, God wants, or God can.
Review your previous answers.

6. The 'So What' or the Next Steps

Now, ask yourself, 'So what?' If what you read is true, how will you apply this? What will you do differently? What has to change?

7. Time to Pray

It is time to pray and ask God to help you. Write down your prayer to God based on what you are learning from today's passage and questions.

1. The Bible: Passage_____ and Date_____

_____/_____/_____

2. The New Thing

What is one new thing that stands out to you in today's passage?
It may be a verse you don't remember reading before.

3. The Wow Factor

What was the most important and impactful thing you read today? What made you say, "Wow! I'm blown away."

4. The Presence of Jesus in the Passage

What points to Jesus and His life in this passage? Does any verse remind you of something Jesus said or the way Jesus lived?

5. The Character of God

Who does God say that He is? Identify attributes from God's character in this passage. A good way to start, is to use words like: God is, God says, God does, God wants, or God can.
Review your previous answers.

6. The 'So What' or the Next Steps

Now, ask yourself, 'So what?' If what you read is true, how will you apply this? What will you do differently? What has to change?

7. Time to Pray

It is time to pray and ask God to help you. Write down your prayer to God based on what you are learning from today's passage and questions.

1. The Bible: Passage_____ and Date_____

_____/_____/_____

2. The New Thing

What is one new thing that stands out to you in today's passage?
It may be a verse you don't remember reading before.

3. The Wow Factor

What was the most important and impactful thing you read today? What made you say, "Wow! I'm blown away."

4. The Presence of Jesus in the Passage

What points to Jesus and His life in this passage? Does any verse remind you of something Jesus said or the way Jesus lived?

5. The Character of God

Who does God say that He is? Identify attributes from God's character in this passage. A good way to start, is to use words like: God is, God says, God does, God wants, or God can.
Review your previous answers.

6. The 'So What' or the Next Steps

Now, ask yourself, 'So what?' If what you read is true, how will you apply this? What will you do differently? What has to change?

7. Time to Pray

It is time to pray and ask God to help you. Write down your prayer to God based on what you are learning from today's passage and questions.

1. The Bible: Passage_____ and Date_____

_____/_____/_____

2. The New Thing

What is one new thing that stands out to you in today's passage?
It may be a verse you don't remember reading before.

3. The Wow Factor

What was the most important and impactful thing you read today? What made you say, "Wow! I'm blown away."

4. The Presence of Jesus in the Passage

What points to Jesus and His life in this passage? Does any verse remind you of something Jesus said or the way Jesus lived?

5. The Character of God

Who does God say that He is? Identify attributes from God's character in this passage. A good way to start, is to use words like: God is, God says, God does, God wants, or God can.
Review your previous answers.

6. The 'So What' or the Next Steps

Now, ask yourself, 'So what?' If what you read is true, how will you apply this? What will you do differently? What has to change?

7. Time to Pray

It is time to pray and ask God to help you. Write down your prayer to God based on what you are learning from today's passage and questions.

1. The Bible: Passage_____ and Date_____

_____/_____/_____

2. The New Thing

What is one new thing that stands out to you in today's passage?
It may be a verse you don't remember reading before.

3. The Wow Factor

What was the most important and impactful thing you read today? What made you say, "Wow! I'm blown away."

4. The Presence of Jesus in the Passage

What points to Jesus and His life in this passage? Does any verse remind you of something Jesus said or the way Jesus lived?

5. The Character of God

Who does God say that He is? Identify attributes from God's character in this passage. A good way to start, is to use words like: God is, God says, God does, God wants, or God can.
Review your previous answers.

6. The 'So What' or the Next Steps

Now, ask yourself, 'So what?' If what you read is true, how will you apply this? What will you do differently? What has to change?

7. Time to Pray

It is time to pray and ask God to help you. Write down your prayer to God based on what you are learning from today's passage and questions.

YOU ARE
PSALM 139:16
fearfully
AND
wonderfully
MADE.

Prayers

1. The Bible: Passage_____ and Date_____

_____/_____/_____

2. The New Thing

What is one new thing that stands out to you in today's passage?
It may be a verse you don't remember reading before.

3. The Wow Factor

What was the most important and impactful thing you read today? What made you say, "Wow! I'm blown away."

4. The Presence of Jesus in the Passage

What points to Jesus and His life in this passage? Does any verse remind you of something Jesus said or the way Jesus lived?

5. The Character of God

Who does God say that He is? Identify attributes from God's character in this passage. A good way to start, is to use words like: God is, God says, God does, God wants, or God can.
Review your previous answers.

6. The 'So What' or the Next Steps

Now, ask yourself, 'So what?' If what you read is true, how will you apply this? What will you do differently? What has to change?

7. Time to Pray

It is time to pray and ask God to help you. Write down your prayer to God based on what you are learning from today's passage and questions.

1. The Bible: Passage_____ and Date_____

_____/_____/_____

2. The New Thing

What is one new thing that stands out to you in today's passage?
It may be a verse you don't remember reading before.

3. The Wow Factor

What was the most important and impactful thing you read today? What made you say, "Wow! I'm blown away."

4. The Presence of Jesus in the Passage

What points to Jesus and His life in this passage? Does any verse remind you of something Jesus said or the way Jesus lived?

5. The Character of God

Who does God say that He is? Identify attributes from God's character in this passage. A good way to start, is to use words like: God is, God says, God does, God wants, or God can.
Review your previous answers.

6. The 'So What' or the Next Steps

Now, ask yourself, 'So what?' If what you read is true, how will you apply this? What will you do differently? What has to change?

7. Time to Pray

It is time to pray and ask God to help you. Write down your prayer to God based on what you are learning from today's passage and questions.

1. The Bible: Passage_____ and Date_____

_____/_____/_____

2. The New Thing

What is one new thing that stands out to you in today's passage?
It may be a verse you don't remember reading before.

3. The Wow Factor

What was the most important and impactful thing you read today? What made you say, "Wow! I'm blown away."

4. The Presence of Jesus in the Passage

What points to Jesus and His life in this passage? Does any verse remind you of something Jesus said or the way Jesus lived?

5. The Character of God

Who does God say that He is? Identify attributes from God's character in this passage. A good way to start, is to use words like: God is, God says, God does, God wants, or God can.
Review your previous answers.

6. The 'So What' or the Next Steps

Now, ask yourself, 'So what?' If what you read is true, how will you apply this? What will you do differently? What has to change?

7. Time to Pray

It is time to pray and ask God to help you. Write down your prayer to God based on what you are learning from today's passage and questions.

1. The Bible: Passage_____ and Date_____

_____/_____/_____

2. The New Thing

What is one new thing that stands out to you in today's passage?
It may be a verse you don't remember reading before.

3. The Wow Factor

What was the most important and impactful thing you read today? What made you say, "Wow! I'm blown away."

4. The Presence of Jesus in the Passage

What points to Jesus and His life in this passage? Does any verse remind you of something Jesus said or the way Jesus lived?

5. The Character of God

Who does God say that He is? Identify attributes from God's character in this passage. A good way to start, is to use words like: God is, God says, God does, God wants, or God can.
Review your previous answers.

6. The 'So What' or the Next Steps

Now, ask yourself, 'So what?' If what you read is true, how will you apply this? What will you do differently? What has to change?

7. Time to Pray

It is time to pray and ask God to help you. Write down your prayer to God based on what you are learning from today's passage and questions.

1. The Bible: Passage_____ and Date_____

_____/_____/_____

2. The New Thing

What is one new thing that stands out to you in today's passage?
It may be a verse you don't remember reading before.

3. The Wow Factor

What was the most important and impactful thing you read today? What made you say, "Wow! I'm blown away."

4. The Presence of Jesus in the Passage

What points to Jesus and His life in this passage? Does any verse remind you of something Jesus said or the way Jesus lived?

5. The Character of God

Who does God say that He is? Identify attributes from God's character in this passage. A good way to start, is to use words like: God is, God says, God does, God wants, or God can.
Review your previous answers.

6. The 'So What' or the Next Steps

Now, ask yourself, 'So what?' If what you read is true, how will you apply this? What will you do differently? What has to change?

7. Time to Pray

It is time to pray and ask God to help you. Write down your prayer to God based on what you are learning from today's passage and questions.

BEST PRAYERS

OF MY LIFE

Psalms 39

Prayer for wisdom and forgiveness

I said to myself, "I will watch what I do and not sin in what I say. I will hold my tongue when the ungodly are around me." But as I stood there in silence—not even speaking of good things—the turmoil within me grew worse. The more I thought about it, the hotter I got, igniting a fire of words: "Lord, remind me how brief my time on earth will be. Remind me that my days are numbered—how fleeting my life is. You have made my life no longer than the width of my hand. My entire lifetime is just a moment to you; at best, each of us is but a breath." We are merely moving shadows, and all our busy rushing ends in nothing. We heap up wealth, not knowing who will spend it. And so, Lord, where do I put my hope? My only hope is in you. Rescue me from my rebellion. Do not let fools mock me. I am silent before you; I won't say a word, for my punishment is from you. But please stop striking me! I am exhausted by the blows from your hand. When you discipline us for our sins, you consume like a moth what is precious to us. Each of us is but a breath. ear my prayer, O Lord! Listen to my cries for help! Don't ignore my tears. For I am your guest—a traveler passing through, as my ancestors were before me. Leave me alone so I can smile again before I am gone and exist no more.

1. The Bible: Passage_____ and Date_____

_____/_____/_____

2. The New Thing

What is one new thing that stands out to you in today's passage?
It may be a verse you don't remember reading before.

3. The Wow Factor

What was the most important and impactful thing you read today? What made you say, "Wow! I'm blown away."

4. The Presence of Jesus in the Passage

What points to Jesus and His life in this passage? Does any verse remind you of something Jesus said or the way Jesus lived?

5. The Character of God

Who does God say that He is? Identify attributes from God's character in this passage. A good way to start, is to use words like: God is, God says, God does, God wants, or God can.
Review your previous answers.

6. The 'So What' or the Next Steps

Now, ask yourself, 'So what?' If what you read is true, how will you apply this? What will you do differently? What has to change?

7. Time to Pray

It is time to pray and ask God to help you. Write down your prayer to God based on what you are learning from today's passage and questions.

1. The Bible: Passage_____ and Date_____

_____/_____/_____

2. The New Thing

What is one new thing that stands out to you in today's passage?
It may be a verse you don't remember reading before.

3. The Wow Factor

What was the most important and impactful thing you read today? What made you say, "Wow! I'm blown away."

4. The Presence of Jesus in the Passage

What points to Jesus and His life in this passage? Does any verse remind you of something Jesus said or the way Jesus lived?

5. The Character of God

Who does God say that He is? Identify attributes from God's character in this passage. A good way to start, is to use words like: God is, God says, God does, God wants, or God can.
Review your previous answers.

6. The 'So What' or the Next Steps

Now, ask yourself, 'So what?' If what you read is true, how will you apply this? What will you do differently? What has to change?

7. Time to Pray

It is time to pray and ask God to help you. Write down your prayer to God based on what you are learning from today's passage and questions.

1. The Bible: Passage_____ and Date_____

_____/_____/_____

2. The New Thing

What is one new thing that stands out to you in today's passage?
It may be a verse you don't remember reading before.

3. The Wow Factor

What was the most important and impactful thing you read today? What made you say, "Wow! I'm blown away."

4. The Presence of Jesus in the Passage

What points to Jesus and His life in this passage? Does any verse remind you of something Jesus said or the way Jesus lived?

5. The Character of God

Who does God say that He is? Identify attributes from God's character in this passage. A good way to start, is to use words like: God is, God says, God does, God wants, or God can.
Review your previous answers.

6. The 'So What' or the Next Steps

Now, ask yourself, 'So what?' If what you read is true, how will you apply this? What will you do differently? What has to change?

7. Time to Pray

It is time to pray and ask God to help you. Write down your prayer to God based on what you are learning from today's passage and questions.

1. The Bible: Passage_____ and Date_____

_____/_____/_____

2. The New Thing

What is one new thing that stands out to you in today's passage?
It may be a verse you don't remember reading before.

3. The Wow Factor

What was the most important and impactful thing you read today? What made you say, "Wow! I'm blown away."

4. The Presence of Jesus in the Passage

What points to Jesus and His life in this passage? Does any verse remind you of something Jesus said or the way Jesus lived?

5. The Character of God

Who does God say that He is? Identify attributes from God's character in this passage. A good way to start, is to use words like: God is, God says, God does, God wants, or God can.
Review your previous answers.

6. The 'So What' or the Next Steps

Now, ask yourself, 'So what?' If what you read is true, how will you apply this? What will you do differently? What has to change?

7. Time to Pray

It is time to pray and ask God to help you. Write down your prayer to God based on what you are learning from today's passage and questions.

1. The Bible: Passage_____ and Date_____

_____/_____/_____

2. The New Thing

What is one new thing that stands out to you in today's passage?
It may be a verse you don't remember reading before.

3. The Wow Factor

What was the most important and impactful thing you read today? What made you say, "Wow! I'm blown away."

4. The Presence of Jesus in the Passage

What points to Jesus and His life in this passage? Does any verse remind you of something Jesus said or the way Jesus lived?

5. The Character of God

Who does God say that He is? Identify attributes from God's character in this passage. A good way to start, is to use words like: God is, God says, God does, God wants, or God can.
Review your previous answers.

6. The 'So What' or the Next Steps

Now, ask yourself, 'So what?' If what you read is true, how will you apply this? What will you do differently? What has to change?

7. Time to Pray

It is time to pray and ask God to help you. Write down your prayer to God based on what you are learning from today's passage and questions.

Jonah 2:1–9

Jonah's prayer

Then Jonah prayed to the LORD his God from inside the fish. He said, "I cried out to the LORD in my great trouble, and he answered me. I called to you from the land of the dead, and LORD, you heard me! You threw me into the ocean depths, and I sank down to the heart of the sea. The mighty waters engulfed me; I was buried beneath your wild and stormy waves. Then I said, 'O LORD, you have driven me from your presence. Yet I will look once more toward your holy Temple.' "I sank beneath the waves, and the waters closed over me. Seaweed wrapped itself around my head. I sank down to the very roots of the mountains. I was imprisoned in the earth, whose gates lock shut forever. But you, O LORD my God, snatched me from the jaws of death! As my life was slipping away, I remembered the LORD. And my earnest prayer went out to you in your holy Temple. Those who worship false gods turn their backs on all God's mercies. But I will offer sacrifices to you with songs of praise, and I will fulfill all my vows. For my salvation comes from the LORD alone."

Be the Light

Matthew 5:14

Prayers

1. The Bible: Passage_____ and Date_____

_____/_____/_____

2. The New Thing

What is one new thing that stands out to you in today's passage?
It may be a verse you don't remember reading before.

3. The Wow Factor

What was the most important and impactful thing you read today? What made you say, "Wow! I'm blown away."

4. The Presence of Jesus in the Passage

What points to Jesus and His life in this passage? Does any verse remind you of something Jesus said or the way Jesus lived?

5. The Character of God

Who does God say that He is? Identify attributes from God's character in this passage. A good way to start, is to use words like: God is, God says, God does, God wants, or God can.
Review your previous answers.

6. The 'So What' or the Next Steps

Now, ask yourself, 'So what?' If what you read is true, how will you apply this? What will you do differently? What has to change?

7. Time to Pray

It is time to pray and ask God to help you. Write down your prayer to God based on what you are learning from today's passage and questions.

1. The Bible: Passage_____ and Date_____

_____/_____/_____

2. The New Thing

What is one new thing that stands out to you in today's passage?
It may be a verse you don't remember reading before.

3. The Wow Factor

What was the most important and impactful thing you read today? What made you say, "Wow! I'm blown away."

4. The Presence of Jesus in the Passage

What points to Jesus and His life in this passage? Does any verse remind you of something Jesus said or the way Jesus lived?

5. The Character of God

Who does God say that He is? Identify attributes from God's character in this passage. A good way to start, is to use words like: God is, God says, God does, God wants, or God can.
Review your previous answers.

6. The 'So What' or the Next Steps

Now, ask yourself, 'So what?' If what you read is true, how will you apply this? What will you do differently? What has to change?

7. Time to Pray

It is time to pray and ask God to help you. Write down your prayer to God based on what you are learning from today's passage and questions.

1. The Bible: Passage_____ and Date_____

_____/_____/_____

2. The New Thing

What is one new thing that stands out to you in today's passage?
It may be a verse you don't remember reading before.

3. The Wow Factor

What was the most important and impactful thing you read today? What made you say, "Wow! I'm blown away."

4. The Presence of Jesus in the Passage

What points to Jesus and His life in this passage? Does any verse remind you of something Jesus said or the way Jesus lived?

5. The Character of God

Who does God say that He is? Identify attributes from God's character in this passage. A good way to start, is to use words like: God is, God says, God does, God wants, or God can.
Review your previous answers.

6. The 'So What' or the Next Steps

Now, ask yourself, 'So what?' If what you read is true, how will you apply this? What will you do differently? What has to change?

7. Time to Pray

It is time to pray and ask God to help you. Write down your prayer to God based on what you are learning from today's passage and questions.

1. The Bible: Passage_____ and Date_____

_____/_____/_____

2. The New Thing

What is one new thing that stands out to you in today's passage?
It may be a verse you don't remember reading before.

3. The Wow Factor

What was the most important and impactful thing you read today? What made you say, "Wow! I'm blown away."

4. The Presence of Jesus in the Passage

What points to Jesus and His life in this passage? Does any verse remind you of something Jesus said or the way Jesus lived?

5. The Character of God

Who does God say that He is? Identify attributes from God's character in this passage. A good way to start, is to use words like: God is, God says, God does, God wants, or God can.
Review your previous answers.

6. The 'So What' or the Next Steps

Now, ask yourself, 'So what?' If what you read is true, how will you apply this? What will you do differently? What has to change?

7. Time to Pray

It is time to pray and ask God to help you. Write down your prayer to God based on what you are learning from today's passage and questions.

1. The Bible: Passage_____ and Date_____

_____/_____/_____

2. The New Thing

What is one new thing that stands out to you in today's passage?
It may be a verse you don't remember reading before.

3. The Wow Factor

What was the most important and impactful thing you read today? What made you say, "Wow! I'm blown away."

4. The Presence of Jesus in the Passage

What points to Jesus and His life in this passage? Does any verse remind you of something Jesus said or the way Jesus lived?

5. The Character of God

Who does God say that He is? Identify attributes from God's character in this passage. A good way to start, is to use words like: God is, God says, God does, God wants, or God can.
Review your previous answers.

6. The 'So What' or the Next Steps

Now, ask yourself, 'So what?' If what you read is true, how will you apply this? What will you do differently? What has to change?

7. Time to Pray

It is time to pray and ask God to help you. Write down your prayer to God based on what you are learning from today's passage and questions.

BEST
PRAYERS

OF
MY
LIFE

Matthew 6:9–13

The Lord's Prayer

Pray like this:

Our Father in heaven,
may your name be kept holy.
May your Kingdom come soon.
May your will be done on earth,
as it is in heaven.
Give us today the food we need,
and forgive us our sins,
as we have forgiven those who sin against us.
And don't let us yield to temptation,
but rescue us from the evil one.

be brave

Psalm 31:24

1. The Bible: Passage_____ and Date_____

_____/_____/_____

2. The New Thing

What is one new thing that stands out to you in today's passage?
It may be a verse you don't remember reading before.

3. The Wow Factor

What was the most important and impactful thing you read today? What made you say, "Wow! I'm blown away."

4. The Presence of Jesus in the Passage

What points to Jesus and His life in this passage? Does any verse remind you of something Jesus said or the way Jesus lived?

BELIEVE IT!

5. The Character of God

Who does God say that He is? Identify attributes from God's character in this passage. A good way to start, is to use words like: God is, God says, God does, God wants, or God can.
Review your previous answers.

6. The 'So What' or the Next Steps

Now, ask yourself, 'So what?' If what you read is true, how will you apply this? What will you do differently? What has to change?

7. Time to Pray

It is time to pray and ask God to help you. Write down your prayer to God based on what you are learning from today's passage and questions.

1. The Bible: Passage_____ and Date_____

_____/_____/_____

2. The New Thing

What is one new thing that stands out to you in today's passage?
It may be a verse you don't remember reading before.

3. The Wow Factor

What was the most important and impactful thing you read today? What made you say, "Wow! I'm blown away."

4. The Presence of Jesus in the Passage

What points to Jesus and His life in this passage? Does any verse remind you of something Jesus said or the way Jesus lived?

5. The Character of God

Who does God say that He is? Identify attributes from God's character in this passage. A good way to start, is to use words like: God is, God says, God does, God wants, or God can.
Review your previous answers.

6. The 'So What' or the Next Steps

Now, ask yourself, 'So what?' If what you read is true, how will you apply this? What will you do differently? What has to change?

7. Time to Pray

It is time to pray and ask God to help you. Write down your prayer to God based on what you are learning from today's passage and questions.

1. The Bible: Passage_____ and Date_____

_____/_____/_____

2. The New Thing

What is one new thing that stands out to you in today's passage?
It may be a verse you don't remember reading before.

3. The Wow Factor

What was the most important and impactful thing you read today? What made you say, "Wow! I'm blown away."

4. The Presence of Jesus in the Passage

What points to Jesus and His life in this passage? Does any verse remind you of something Jesus said or the way Jesus lived?

5. The Character of God

Who does God say that He is? Identify attributes from God's character in this passage. A good way to start, is to use words like: God is, God says, God does, God wants, or God can.
Review your previous answers.

6. The 'So What' or the Next Steps

Now, ask yourself, 'So what?' If what you read is true, how will you apply this? What will you do differently? What has to change?

7. Time to Pray

It is time to pray and ask God to help you. Write down your prayer to God based on what you are learning from today's passage and questions.

1. The Bible: Passage_____ and Date_____

_____/_____/_____

2. The New Thing

What is one new thing that stands out to you in today's passage?
It may be a verse you don't remember reading before.

3. The Wow Factor

What was the most important and impactful thing you read today? What made you say, "Wow! I'm blown away."

4. The Presence of Jesus in the Passage

What points to Jesus and His life in this passage? Does any verse remind you of something Jesus said or the way Jesus lived?

5. The Character of God

Who does God say that He is? Identify attributes from God's character in this passage. A good way to start, is to use words like: God is, God says, God does, God wants, or God can.
Review your previous answers.

6. The 'So What' or the Next Steps

Now, ask yourself, 'So what?' If what you read is true, how will you apply this? What will you do differently? What has to change?

7. Time to Pray

It is time to pray and ask God to help you. Write down your prayer to God based on what you are learning from today's passage and questions.

1. The Bible: Passage_____ and Date_____

_____/_____/_____

2. The New Thing

What is one new thing that stands out to you in today's passage?
It may be a verse you don't remember reading before.

3. The Wow Factor

What was the most important and impactful thing you read today? What made you say, "Wow! I'm blown away."

4. The Presence of Jesus in the Passage

What points to Jesus and His life in this passage? Does any verse remind you of something Jesus said or the way Jesus lived?

5. The Character of God

Who does God say that He is? Identify attributes from God's character in this passage. A good way to start, is to use words like: God is, God says, God does, God wants, or God can.
Review your previous answers.

6. The 'So What' or the Next Steps

Now, ask yourself, 'So what?' If what you read is true, how will you apply this? What will you do differently? What has to change?

7. Time to Pray

It is time to pray and ask God to help you. Write down your prayer to God based on what you are learning from today's passage and questions.

Ephesians 1:16–19

Prayer for spiritual wisdom

I have not stopped thanking God for you. I pray for you constantly, asking God, the glorious Father of our Lord Jesus Christ, to give you spiritual wisdom[a] and insight so that you might grow in your knowledge of God. I pray that your hearts will be flooded with light so that you can understand the confident hope he has given to those he called—his holy people who are his rich and glorious inheritance. I also pray that you will understand the incredible greatness of God's power for us who believe him. This is the same mighty power

Prayers

Notes

Be the Light

Matthew 5:14

Notes

Be the Light
the
Matthew 5:14

Notes

Be the Light

Matthew 5:14

Notes

Be the Light

Matthew 5:14

Notes

Be the Light

Matthew 5:14

Notes

Be the Light

Matthew 5:14

Notes

_____

_____

_____

_____

_____

_____

_____

_____

_____

_____

_____

_____

_____

_____

_____

Be the Light

Matthew 5:14

Notes

Be the Light

Matthew 5:14

Notes

Be the Light

Matthew 5:14

Notes

Be the Light
Matthew 5:14

Notes

Be the Light

Matthew 5:14

Notes

Be the Light

Matthew 5:14

DEVOTIONAL PRAYER BOOK
FOR
Women

100 DAYS EXPERIENCING GOD
THROUGH A 7-STEP DAILY BIBLE STUDY

www.ingramcontent.com/pod-product-compliance
Lightning Source LLC
Chambersburg PA
CBHW041111120626

46547CB00019B/2666